ON ELOQUENCE

On Eloquence

DENIS DONOGHUE

Yale University Press   New Haven and London

Set in by Caslon by Tseng Information Systems, Inc.
Printed in the United States of America.

Library of Congress Cataloging-in-Publication Data
Donoghue, Denis.
On eloquence / Denis Donoghue.
p. cm.
Includes bibliographical references (p.   ) and index.
ISBN 978-0-300-12541-2 (alk. paper)
1. Oratory. 2. Eloquence. 3. Eloquence in literature. I. Title.
PN4129.15.D66 2008
808.5'1—dc22
2007016897

A catalogue record for this book is available from the British Library.

∞ The paper in this book meets the guidelines
for permanence and durability of the Committee
on Production Guidelines for Book Longevity of
the Council on Library Resources.

10 9 8 7 6 5 4 3 2 1

For Frances

Contents

I

Taking Notes

Eloquence is simply the end of art, and is thus its essence. Even the poorest art is eloquent, but in a poor way, with less intensity, until this aspect is obscured by others fattening upon its leanness.
— *Kenneth Burke,* Counter-Statement

We are all prepared to applaud eloquence when it is employed in the service of truth, but when it is turned the other way, should we continue to admire it anyway—although now as the display of splendid technique and an instance of inspired rodomontade?
— *William H. Gass,* Tests of Time

I

Adam named things:

> And out of the ground the LORD GOD formed every
> beast of the field, and every fowl of the air; and
> brought *them* unto Adam to see what he would call
> them; and whatsoever Adam called every living
> creature, that *was* the name thereof.
>
> And Adam gave names to all cattle, and to the
> fowl of the air, and to every beast of the field.
> (Gen. 2:19–20)[1]

As a result, the referential act of language is deemed to be its first duty. That is a dove. That is a sparrow. That is a lamb. But as language developed in complex relation to consciousness, it discovered possibilities beyond reference. Abstractions are among those discoveries. You can't point to something and say "that is beauty" or "that is truth" or "that is objectivity." In some degree, language becomes autonomous: thought "ceases to be practice."[2] In some degree, because it is never entirely detached from things and its responsibility toward them. *Alice in Wonderland* and *Finnegans Wake* are nearly detached from them, but not quite: they tell stories, and the stories are related, however deviantly, to the world or worlds we hold in common. But we take pleasure in eloquence that is not merely or completely referential. In "The Convalescent," a chapter of the third book of *Thus Spoke Zarathustra*, Zarathustra remains in his cave for seven days till he recovers from his collapse. Then he raises himself, takes up an apple, smells it, and finds it delightful. At this point the animals urge him to come into the world and speak. When he does, he speaks about language:

> How lovely it is that there are words and sounds. Are not words and sounds rainbows and illusive bridges between things which are eternally apart? But all sounds make us forget this; how lovely it is that we forget. . . . Are not words and sounds given to things so that man can renew himself through things? Speech is a beautiful folly: by means of it, man dances over all things. How sweet is all speech; [how sweet] all the illusion of sounds! With sounds our love dances on many-coloured rainbows.[3]

The dancing of speech is eloquence: the aim of a dance is not to get from one part of the village green or the stage to another, it is to create and embody yet another form of life beyond the already known forms of it. In dancing, the dancers enjoy the certitude of being alive in their bodies. That is eloquence. "Art is magic delivered from the lie of being truth."[4] Eloquence, as Geoffrey Hartman has said of art and might say of play, "is a reminder, both forceful and delightful, of unbound energies—anarchic, self-pleasuring—behind and within codification."⁵ Eloquence does not vex its own creation. Delighting in difference, it opposes—but without argument—the otherwise omnivorous culture of the same. We value it as a sign of such freedom as we are ever likely to enjoy.

It is commonly assumed that eloquence is a form or a subset of rhetoric, a means to rhetorical ends. That is not true. Rhetoric has an aim, to move people to do one thing rather than another. Hitler's *Mein Kampf* is a work of rhetoric. So is *The Communist Manifesto*. So are Stanley Fish's *Is There a Text in This Class?* and Jacques Derrida's *De la grammatologie*. So is every papal encyclical, every homily, every speech in Parliament or Congress. A speech or an essay may be eloquent, but if it is, the eloquence is incidental to its aim. Eloquence, as distinct from rhetoric, has no aim: it is a play of words or other expressive means. It is a gift to be enjoyed in appreciation and practice. The main attribute of eloquence is gratuitousness: its place in the world is to be without place or function, its mode is to be intrinsic. Like beauty, it claims only the privilege of being a grace note in the culture that permits it.

Normally, we recognize an eloquent event as a flare of expression, an excess or superabundance of its qualities. But there are several kinds of eloquence. Some are thrilling in their audacity—they are prophetic, magical, sublime, we futilely say: if we tire of them or are not in the mood to appreciate their excesses, we say that they are pretentious, as Coleridge spoke of "a nimiety, too-muchness." Shakespeare's sonnets are such a case. But there is also an eloquence of least means, as in the shock of understatement, where one's excitement arises from the surprise of finding something said so barely yet so definitively. In Eliot's "Marina" no one could have anticipated the "new ships" in "The awakened, lips parted, the hope, the new ships," even though the first part of the stanza spoke of "The rigging weak and the canvas rotten." "New" is not exorbitant. George Herbert's first "Prayer," after much experimental listing, ends with "something understood." Vaughan's "World" begins: "I saw eternity the other night." Imagine: just the other night, and such a thing to see. Wordsworth's "Michael" nearly ends: "And never lifted up a single stone." "Ignorant" is a common or garden word, transformed to eloquence in Arnold's "Where ignorant armies clash by night." Context accounts for much in these instances from Arnold, Wordsworth, and the other writers, but when eloquence arises, we recognize it as a discovery within the medium itself, free of every rhetorical motive, an expressive act come upon as if by the way and with no intent of its being sought. To appreciate eloquence is an intelligent pleasure; we stand aside from its manifestations sufficiently to enjoy them. Eloquence therefore is exempt—or should be—from the imputations that hang over rhetorical acts and consequences. It puts rhetoric to shame—persuasion, propaganda, nudging, forcing—for its vulgarity of purpose, its forensic disgusts. Eloquence does not kill people.

II

The question of the English language, in its bearing upon eloquence, theory and ideology, did not arise until well into the sixteenth century. Till then, native speakers of the language and scholars of it alike agreed that English was rude, if not barbarous, by comparison with Hebrew, Greek, Latin, Spanish, French, and Italian. The achievements of Chaucer, Gower, and Lydgate were regarded as making a closed chapter in the history of the language, having little bearing on the development of the vernacular.[6] But two attitudes were available on the question. One: you could hold that English, a homespun thing, was poor but honest, a serviceable language for use in common life and local relations, even if it was limited to those practices. At least it kept itself free from the sophistications of Europe; it did not need to be eloquent so long as it was decent. George Chapman wrote in 1575: "I have rather regarde to make our native language commendable in it selfe, than gay with the feathers of straunge birdes."[7] Two, the modern attitude: you could hold that as long as the language was content with its rural honesty, it could have no access to the new knowledges of science, medicine, mathematics, geography, philosophy, and theology brought forward by the Renaissance. The crucial issue was *copie (copia)*, the language needed a larger supply of words, many of them new, among which one could choose. After the publication of Tyndale's *New Testament* in 1526 (revised in 1534), Coverdale's Bible in 1535, the *Great Bible* in 1539, the *Book of Common Prayer* in 1549, the Geneva Bible in 1560, Foxe's *Actes and Monumentes* in 1563, the Douay version of the Old Testament in 1609, and the King James Bible in 1611, it was impossible to take the English language for granted. The view that eventually prevailed was that English must be brought to a condition of refinement and eloquence at least equal to that of the old and the modern languages.

The devices available for this purpose were mainly translations of the Bible and the secular classics of Greece and Rome; commentaries on the rhetorics of Aristotle, Cicero, Quintilian, Erasmus, and other authorities; translations of popular Italian fiction for entertainment and for use in the Elizabethan theater; incorporation of classical figures of thought and speech; neologisms, new coinages derived from old words or from foreign words and more useful for new needs: these words would seem awkward for a time, but they would gradually be domesticated and in the end would appear as native as any other words; and the use of words and music together in English song. It was also often thought—eloquence confounded with rhetoric—that eloquence was not merely pretty pictures, and that it was necessary to study "the practice of eloquence as the practice of power."[8] By about 1580 these several devices were successful to the extent that English was deemed to be just as eloquent as any other language. The fact that a language could be used to serve evil ends as well as good ones was for the most part ignored.[9]

But as soon as the language reached perfection, inevitably it declined, fell into sophistication, corruption in manners and behavior leading to corruption in speech. After the Civil War, the Restoration of Charles II, the Revolution of 1688–89 that installed William of Orange on the throne, and the Act of Settlement (1701), a new motive arose that had considerable bearing on the status of eloquence in the English language. There must never again be a Civil War. Party politics was inevitable, but it should be possible to appeal beyond faction, religious conflicts, and the divisions of Whig and Tory to the image of a true-born Englishman, type of national unity, to whom party was a secondary consideration. Religious observance might be replaced by table manners, the Act of Uniformity by the elegant disposition of knives, forks, and spoons. Money, class, and taste might hold a society together in peace, making up for the divisiveness of religion. (For much the same reason in the United States after the Civil War, it was crucial to appeal beyond the conflicts of North and South to the sentiment of "the American people," an entity hard to define then as now.) In Britain the attempt to adumbrate a true-born Englishman depended upon several facilities: secular modes of agreement such as the cultivation of taste, the projection of Culture as the highest value to which it was possible to aspire; the presentation of manners as more persuasive than laws; the privileging of middle-class values and aspirations; the gradual extension of suffrage to include more and more of that class; the growing prestige of natural science, embodied in the activities of the Royal Society; the development of a middle style of speech and writing predicated on science and civil conversation as distinct alike from the low style of satire and from the high style of epic and the sublime. In the first years of the eighteenth century, these motives expressed themselves (not without fear of censorship and prosecution) in the familiar essay of Addison and Steele, the gentlemanly report in natural science, and the often-anonymous or pseudonymous social or political pamphlet. The high style, natural home of eloquence, might still be practiced, but it could easily be dismissed as picturesque or indeed ridiculous. This continues to be a risk. The wartime speeches of Winston Churchill, the high eloquence of John F. Kennedy, Martin Luther King Jr., and Jesse Jackson—these are protected from irony by a residual sense of the emotions of crisis, war, and assassination. Without such sentiments—some of them annually revived, as on Martin Luther King Day—the speeches would sink into the lore of their times and be smiled away as quaint or operatic.

By the beginning of the eighteenth century, English was thought to be a splendidly expressive language, but some critics of it were disappointed by its public performances. In 1742 David Hume asked, in an essay on eloquence, why modern Britain was so inferior in that regard to the Greece of Demosthenes and the Rome of Cicero. No member of the two houses of Parliament, he claimed, had attained "much beyond a mediocrity" in his speeches. Hume speculated that "the multiplicity and intricacy of laws" in modern Britain was "a discouragement to eloquence." A modern lawyer could merely negotiate the thickets as best he could: eloquence would not help him. There was also the consideration that modern society was too rational to tolerate the standard rhetorical gestures:

It may be pretended, that the decline of eloquence is owing to the superior good sense of the moderns, who reject with disdain all those rhetorical tricks employed to seduce the judges, and will admit of nothing but solid argument in any debate of deliberation.

National constitution came into the question, too:

There are some circumstances in the English temper and genius, which are disadvantageous to the progress of eloquence, and render all attempts of that kind more dangerous and difficult among them, than among any other nation in the universe. The English are conspicuous for *good sense,* which makes them very jealous of any attempts to deceive them, by the flowers of rhetoric and elocution. They are also peculiarly *modest;* which makes them consider it as a piece of arrogance to offer any thing but reason to public assemblies, or attempt to guide them by passion or fancy. I may, perhaps, be allowed to add that the people in general are not remarkable for delicacy of taste, or for sensibility to the charms of the Muses.

According to Hume, Britain chose the Attic rather than the Asiatic style of eloquence, "calm, elegant, and subtile, which instructed the reason more than affected the passions, and never raised its tone above argument or common discourse."[10] In the essay "Of National Characters" he remarked with satisfaction a cooling of the passions in religious conviction:

Not to insist upon the great difference between the present possessors of Britain, and those before the Roman conquest, we may observe, that our ancestors, a few centuries ago, were sunk into the most abject superstition. Last century they were inflamed with the most furious enthusiasm, and are now settled into the most cool indifference, with regard to religious matters, that is to be found in any nation of the world.[11]

But in the essay on eloquence Hume says, without offering many reasons for his recommendation, that it would be good for Britain to restore "the pathetic" and "the sublime," notable qualities of the old eloquence. "Now, banish the pathetic from public discourses, and you reduce the speakers merely to modern eloquence; that is, to good sense, delivered in proper expressions."[12] Apparently he thought that British culture was at risk of becoming phlegmatic, despite local disputes of Whig and Tory that kept it at least intermittently awake.

No one thought that the language was secure. In the preface to *A Dictionary of the English Language* (1755), Samuel Johnson noted:

> When I took the first survey of my undertaking, I found our speech copious without order, and energetick without rules: wherever I turned my view, there was perplexity to be disentangled, and confusion to be regulated; choice was to be made out of boundless variety, without any established principle of selection; adulterations were to be detected, without a settled test of purity; and modes of expression to be rejected or received, without the suffrages of any writers of classical reputation or acknowledged authority.

Judged by Johnson's criteria, the language was in decline. He wanted to "ascertain" and "fix" it at the point now reached in his pronouncements upon it, his receptions and rejections, and to keep it fixed there indefinitely. Jonathan Swift expressed the same desire. Johnson said:

> Language is only the instrument of science, and words are but the signs of ideas: I wish, however, that the instrument might be less apt to decay, and that signs might be permanent, like the things which they denote.

Johnson thought that English had reached its best form of itself—*"the wells of English undefiled"*—in the age of Elizabeth, and he took most of his words from that source:

> I have fixed *Sidney*'s work for the boundary, beyond which I make few excursions. From the authours which rose in the time of *Elizabeth*, a speech might be formed adequate to all the purposes of use and elegance. If the language of theology were extracted from *Hooker* and the translation of the Bible; the terms of natural knowledge from *Bacon;* the phrases of policy, war, and navigation from *Raleigh;* the dialect of poetry and fiction from *Spenser* and *Sidney;* and the diction of common life from *Shakespeare,* few ideas would be lost to mankind, for want of *English* words, in which they might be expressed.

But such perfection cannot be held. Changes must come, and with them corruption: from commerce; from the raising of the cultural level of the people to a degree "polished by arts, and classed by subordination, where one part of the community is sustained and accommodated by the labour of the other"; from the mixture of two languages, such that the people of England could be reduced to babble a dialect of French; from frequency of translation, since "no book was ever turned from one language into another, without imparting something of its native idiom; this is the mischievous and comprehensive innovation; single words may enter by thousands, and the fabrick of the tongue continue the same, but new phraseology changes much at once; it alters not the single stones of the building, but the order of the columns."[13]

Johnson didn't think he could do much to repair these corruptions. "Tongues, like governments, have a natural tendency to degeneration." Still, "let us make some struggles for our language."[14]

Since the middle of the eighteenth century, fears for the health of the English language have been provoked more by instances of decadence than those of penury. Two passages, from Wordsworth and Coleridge, are sufficient to make the point. Wordsworth's preface to the second edition of *Lyrical Ballads* (1800) resumes many such complaints:

> For a multitude of causes, unknown to former times, are now acting with a combined force to blunt the discriminating powers of the mind, and, unfitting it for all voluntary exertion, to reduce it to a state of almost savage torpor. The most effective of these causes are the great national events which are daily taking place, and the increasing accumulation of men in cities, where the uniformity of their occupations produces a craving for extraordinary incident, which the rapid communication of intelligence hourly gratifies. To this tendency of life and manners the literature and theatrical exhibitions of the country have conformed themselves. The invaluable works of our elder writers, I had almost said the works of Shakspeare and Milton,

are driven into neglect by frantic novels, sickly and stupid German Tragedies, and deluges of idle and extravagant stories in verse.[15]

"The rapid communication of intelligence": meaning news-papers, as today it would mean television and the Internet. "A craving for extraordinary incident" would correspond to our "reality" television. "Sickly and stupid German Tragedies": our pulp fiction, the best-seller list, in Henry James's phrase "trash triumphant."

The second passage is from chapter 22 of *Biographia Literaria*, in which Coleridge considers the defects and merits of Wordsworth's poetry and their particular bearing "in an age of corrupt eloquence":

> In prose I doubt whether it be even possible to preserve our style wholly unalloyed by the vicious phraseology which meets us every where, from the sermon to the newspaper, from the harangue of the legislator to the speech from the convivial chair, announcing a *toast* or sentiment. Our chains rattle, even while we are complaining of them.[16]

The problem was not to make English copious but to make it honorable. English ought to be kept up, a project furthered by many poets from Wordsworth, Coleridge, Keats, and Hopkins to Geoffrey Hill. It was taken up, too, by philologists and lexicographers, the Oxford English Dictionary their most telling achievement in historical recovery. The problem was to reconcile several concurrent demands: the style of commerce, the *translatio studii* of the classics at a time when it was yielding to the vernacular as the language of progress, the force of Enlightenment and its ideally univocal style.

III

It has occurred to me, during the past several years as a teacher of English, Irish, and American literature at New York University, that the qualities of writing I care about are increasingly hard to expound: aesthetic finesse, beauty, eloquence, style, form, imagination, fiction, the architecture of a sentence, the bearing of rhyme, pleasure, "how to do things with words." It has become harder to persuade students that these are real places of interest and value in a poem, a play, a novel, or an essay in the *New Yorker*. Other issues have asserted themselves. "What we find in the universities," as Hartman says, "is a rising demand for a didactic approach, for advocacy teaching that uses art in a cause. Criticism renounces its freedom and returns to the missionary position."[17] The politics of Yeats's last poems — was he a Fascist? Conrad versus Chinua Achebe — was Conrad complicit with Imperialism? T. S. Eliot's anti-Semitism: The Case of "Burbank with a Baedeker: Bleistein with a Cigar." V. S. Naipaul and His Capitulation to English Culture. Nadine Gordimer and the New Africa. The Printing Press and the Rise of Nationalism. These and many similar topics are in high standing in departments of English, but I am not much interested in them, because they lead me away from the literature I care for toward serious issues that are treated well enough by political commentators in books and magazines. What are the ideological implications of *King Lear?* That is not, in fact, a bad question. The language of the play has much to say about life in terms of price, value, and audits.[18] A small moral of its story is that a king should not abdicate — divest himself of his holdings — unless he has to, and if he abdicates without need he should not fool himself into thinking that he can retain as a "reservation" "the name, and all th' additions to a king." But a better question is: how did Shakespeare turn "the quality of nothing" into *King Lear*? How did he write the play, and what are the marks of it? These are questions in aesthetics, which point "to a value present beyond any appropriation of it by current utilitarian ideas."[19] How has Shakespeare worded the play? Further questions I take pleasure in: how does William H. Gass compose a sentence; how did Guy Davenport make a paragraph; how did Yeats find that particular way of writing "No Second Troy"; how did Calvino construct *Invisible Cities*?

IV

As a case in point: suppose we are reading one of Whitman's most eloquent passages, the last part of "Out of the Cradle Endlessly Rocking" (in its final version):

> A word then, (for I will conquer it,)
> The word final, superior to all,
> Subtle, sent up—what is it?—I listen;
> Are you whispering it, and have been all the time, you
>   sea-waves?
> Is that it from your liquid rims and wet sands?
>
> Whereto answering, the sea,
> Delaying not, hurrying not,
> Whisper'd me through the night, and very plainly before
>   daybreak,
> Lisp'd to me the low and delicious word death,
> And again death, death, death, death,
> Hissing melodious, neither like the bird nor like my
>   arous'd child's heart,
> But edging near as privately for me rustling at my feet,
> Creeping thence steadily up to my ears and laving me
>   softly all over,
> Death, death, death, death, death.

Which I do not forget,
But fuse the song of my dusky demon and brother,
That he sang to me in the moonlight on Paumanok's
  gray beach,
With the thousand responsive songs at random,
My own songs awaked from that hour,
And with them the key, the word up from the waves,
The word of the sweetest song and all songs,
That strong and delicious word which, creeping to my
  feet,
(Or like some old crone rocking the cradle, swathed in
  sweet garments, bending aside,)
The sea whisper'd me.[20]

I don't offer a full reading. I note only that the "dusky demon and brother" is given earlier in the poem as the mockingbird; demon and brother because it is not yet clear whether the delivered word *death* is entirely creative or not—though in the end it is, "the word up from the waves," death being in Whitman's terms a part of life. Twenty lines back, Whitman wondered, in the guise of "the boy's soul," whether the bird was "Demon or bird!"—an allusion to Poe's "The Raven," as Guy Davenport has noted, where Poe's man of sorrows knows that the raven is a prophet but not whether it is "bird or devil":

> "Prophet!" said I, "thing of evil! Prophet still, if bird or
>   devil!—
> Whether Tempter sent, or whether tempest tossed thee
>   here ashore,
> Desolate yet all undaunted . . .[21]

In the end, Whitman is prepared to accept that the bird is demon—that is, *daimon*—and brother and to fuse its song with his own.

The verse is free, in the sense that one line is related to the next not by a count of syllables or spoken stresses but by affiliations of breath and cadence. As in music, there are motifs, three in particular, "death," "song," and "word." Reading the passage with students, I'd try to indicate the kind of attention one might pay to the last line and the various forms of the verb *to whisper*. In the first section, "Are you whispering it?" the verb is transitive, *it* standing for the word soon revealed as *death*. In the second, "Whisper'd me through the night," it seems to be transitive, but if it is, its object is *me*, a cogent reading since the sea has taken part with the bird in the transformation of boy into bard, one form of expressiveness creating another. But Whitman almost erases that reading in the next line by "Lisp'd to me the low and delicious word death," where the effect is to make the preceding *Whisper'd* intransitive, a version of "Whisper'd [to] me," no direct object of the sentence being given. In the last section, the grammar eventually has "That strong and delicious word" as object of *whisper'd*, so the last line should be read as if its logic entailed "The sea whisper'd the word death to me." But the effect of the long interpolated line about the old crone is to put the final verb at such a remove from its object that the line it inhabits takes on a high degree of independence. We are nearly authorized to read "The sea whisper'd me" as if the entire poem culminated in this act of conjuring, projection, or creation. There is at least an equivocation between *death* and *me* as object of the whispering, even if it is resolved in the end in favor of *death* as the encompassing term. Angus Fletcher has remarked of such passages in Whitman that "the style, instead of being natural or transparent, is designedly opaque, but in a special sense: the aim is to produce a language that, instead of communicating something, reveals its own elemental laws and rhythms."[22] "Instead of communicating something" restricts the possibilities unnecessarily. The passage I've quoted communicates a great deal. But Fletcher's emphasis on the language revealing, as a chief aim while not the sole one, "its own elemental laws and rhythms" is just. If so, every line of Whitman's poetry is autobiographical, since it is adjectival to his sense of himself, however that is to be construed in terms of process and change. The lines "communicate something," but the something is not accorded independent existence, as if it were separate from the voice that invoked it. The voice sings itself, its own song. This is subjective poetry in the sense that the objects summoned forth minister to the subject, the speaker. The speaker is to a remarkable extent at one with the language as it performs itself. Every poem of Whitman's is a song of myself, though the self declared in performance is a form of feeling operative for the occasion rather than a particular event deemed to be definitive and irrefutable. This suggests that one should read Whitman's poems as trajectories that declare themselves in their own forms and values, and postpone as long as possible—ideally forever—the temptation to "go outside" the poems in search of political, social, sexual, or other intimations. *Leaves of Grass* is a phenomenology of styles achieving themselves while at the same time reflecting on their processes. The poems are autobiographical; a self—at any moment shadowy and equivocal—commits itself to its determination within the language and by the language alone.

I would like to find that students who elect to take a course in modern poetry would be interested in this kind of reading, whether they call it New Criticism or not. Some are interested. But there are several forces in our society that work against such an interest. The main one is the premature concentration, even in general education, on the knowledge and capacities necessary for entry to professional careers. These careers are crucial, but not at the moment the students graduate from high school. It is regrettable that undergraduate education is already turned toward the professional and managerial skills on which students will depend for a livelihood. Those skills do not include eloquence or an appreciation of eloquence: each profession has its own ways of speech, corresponding to its pragmatic purposes and values. The idea that undergraduates should enjoy three or four years of "liberal education"—education in subjects not directed immediately toward jobs—has evidently lost much of its force. In "On the Teaching of Modern Literature," Lionel Trilling asked whether the study of the past, precisely because it is the past, might not provide "that quiet place at which a young man might stand for a few years, at least a little beyond the competing attitudes and generalizations of the present"—

> at least a little beyond the contemporary problems which he is told he can master only by means of attitudes and generalizations, that quiet place in which he can be silent, in which he can *know* something—in what year the Parthenon was begun, the order of battle at Trafalgar, how Linear B was deciphered: almost anything at all that has nothing to do with the talkative and attitudinizing present, anything at all but variations on the accepted formulations about *anxiety,* and *urban society,* and *alienation,* and *Gemeinschaft* and *Gesellschaft,* all the matter of the academic disciplines which are founded upon the modern self-consciousness and the modern self-pity.[23]

Students would soon enough concentrate on the knowledges required for their careers in medicine, law, business administration, journalism, economics, and the other professions. Trilling's urging in that frantic sentence has had no visible effect. It could not win, against the cultural indifference to the past and the corresponding insistence that only the present and the near future are to be attended to. Instant messaging, the Internet, and the cell phone are the favored instruments of that attention.

In the general culture, there are other causes of indifference to eloquence. I have nothing new or wise to say about the anti-intellectual prejudice in America; the frail hold that avant-garde art and experimental writing have on contemporary culture, where they are soon domesticated to become artifacts like any other; the infatuation with professional sport on TV; the social adjudications of style and taste which are vested in possessions—one's choices among things to be bought, the shopping mall offering itself as Universal Exhibition; the triumph of middlebrow culture as the form in which the nearest simulacrum of high culture is accepted by the masses; the acceptance of the TV interview as vehicle of serious public speech.[24] These cultural practices are well understood, grieved over by a few cultural critics, and accepted in practice by multitudes, myself often (I am sorry to say) included.

Meanwhile, we have our topic, accompanied by a few preliminary admonitions. Eloquence, as Michael Baxandall justly says of beauty, is a less verifiable category than wealth.[25] I'll not offer to verify it. Eloquence also comes in flashes, sometimes in a phrase or two: "Stay me with flagons, comfort me with apples: for I *am* sick of love" (Song of Sol. 2:5). Sometimes it breaks forth in a single word. Dante's "Tanto gentile" has as its context the other poems and the prose of the *Vita Nuova*, but it lives on the uncanny eloquence of its last word:

> un spirito soave pien d'amore,
> che va dicendo a l'anima: Sospira.

(and from her face there seems to move a gentle spirit full of love that keeps saying to the soul: "Sigh.")[26] It is not surprising that one's responsiveness to a single word incurs a suspicion of decadence. "A style of decadence," Havelock Ellis wrote in an essay on Paul Bourget, "is one in which the unity of the book is decomposed to give place to the independence of the page, in which the page is decomposed to give place to the independence of the phrase, and the phrase to give place to the independence of the word."[27] I can't dispel that suspicion in general; a feeling for eloquence is likely to be gratified by sudden gestures, flares of spirit, words breaking free from every expectation, audacities of diction and syntax. I can't promise that all the instances I quote will be found not guilty. This book, I am pleased to note, is full of quotations. It can't be bad to enlighten its pages with flashes from many sources, noises, sounds, and sweet airs that give delight and hurt not.

2

The Latin Factor

I

The secondary school I attended, as a day-boy, was the Christian Brothers' in Newry, County Down, Northern Ireland, about five miles from our home in Warrenpoint. I traveled the miles by train, bus, or, in agreeable weather, by bicycle. The teachers were an order of brothers, not priests. Once a priest, always a priest, but a brother could leave the order when he chose. So long as he remained, he lived in a community of his colleagues and was bound by vows of poverty, chastity, and obedience. The Congregation of the Christian Brothers was founded by Edmund Ignatius Rice in Waterford in 1802 with the mission of giving Catholic boys a suitable education—primary, secondary, and technical—at little or no cost to their parents. Gradually, the Brothers set up schools throughout Ireland and eventually in some towns in the United States. They received formal approval from Pope Pius VII in 1820. But their social standing in Ireland was low; they did not have the *aura* of priests. In *A Portrait of the Artist as a Young Man,* when Stephen Dedalus has to be withdrawn from Clongowes Wood College—an expensive Jesuit boarding school in County Kildare that his father can no longer afford—the question of sending him to one of the Christian Brothers' schools in Dublin arises, but his mother and father are agreed in disliking the notion:

> Christian brothers be damned! said Mr Dedalus.
> Is it with Paddy Stink and Mickey Mud? No, let

him stick to the jesuits in God's name since he began with them. They'll be of service to him in after years. Those are the fellows that can get you a position.[1]

My father, a police sergeant in the Royal Ulster Constabulary, did not share Simon Dedalus's social prejudice; he evidently thought the Christian Brothers would suit me and my brother Tim well enough, and I agreed with him. The possibility of my being sent off to a boarding school for misbehavior was an occasional threat, but an empty one: my father could not have risen to its fees. Besides, the likelihood of sharing a desk with Paddy Stink or Mickey Mud did not trouble me.

The secondary education offered by the Christian Brothers was predicated on Latin, the language of the Roman Catholic Church and of the Mass. I was audible in Latin before I understood a word of it. In St. Peter's Church, Warrenpoint, I was an altar boy, so I learned by rote the Latin responses for Mass. When the priest stood at the foot of the altar and intoned the words "Introibo ad altare Dei," I was ready with the response, "Ad Deum qui laetificat juventutem meum." Later, when I learned the English translation, I thought it a feeble thing: "I will go up to the altar of God, to God who gives joy to my youth." There was little joy in that giving, compared to the polysyllabic thrill of "laetificat juventutem meum." The words consorted with the gong I struck, at appropriate moments during the Mass, letting the reverberation continue for two or three seconds before stilling it with my free hand. It did not occur to me until many years later when I read *Ulysses* that the change of one syllable from Deum to Deam would render the response disgraceful, a change effected by Stephen Dedalus, at the cost of ruining the pronoun, in the "Circe" chapter when he cries out to Lynch's "Where are we going?": "Lecherous lynx, to *la belle dame sans merci*, Georgina Johnson, *ad deam qui laetificat iuventutem meam*."[2] I'm afraid I attended to the sounds of Latin rather than to the sense. The choir in our local church sang mostly the hymns of Saint Thomas Aquinas, especially *Pange lingua gloriosi*, *O salutaris Hostia*, and *Adoro Te devote*, sometimes in corrupt texts. I gather that the first line of *Adoro Te devote* should end with "latens veritas"—the hidden Truth, not "latens deitas," the hidden divinity, but we did not advert to the theological difference, large as it is.[3] We sang the *Pange lingua*, in Aquinas's version, on Holy Thursday in the procession to the sanctuary where the Blessed Sacrament was kept until Good Friday. I delighted in the play of words in "Nobis datus, nobis natus" even though I did not understand the particular words in play. Much later I heard of a more profound play of words in the sixth-century version of the *Pange lingua* by Venantius Fortunatus, which has one stanza celebrating the Cross of the Crucifixion:

> Crux fidelis, inter omnes arbor una nobilis
> Nulla silva talem profert fronde flore germine;
> Dulce lignum dulce clavo dulce pondus sustinens.

"Faithful Cross, among all others a noble tree / No woodland brought forth such a leaf, a flower, a shoot; / Sweet tree sustaining a sweet burden with a sweet nail."[4]

When I was informally promoted to the rank of soloist, I brought my ardent boy soprano voice to the *Stabat Mater Dolorosa* as part of the Stations of the Cross. I often sang the *Panis Angelicus* of Aquinas in César Franck's opulent setting, but I did not ask myself what the poet meant by "Dat panis caelicus figuris terminum": The heavenly bread has put an end to figures. Many years later, I found the sentence elucidated by Hugh Kenner:

> The heavenly nourishment (bread and flesh at once)
> has put an end to "figures." Figures can only say,
> "This is 'like' what cannot be shown; what you see
> is an emblem." No more of that now: no more of
> *this* making shift to "represent" *that*. We have the
> gift of the Eucharist, which *is* what it represents.
> Polyhedral Being is gathered together now, the
> faces different yet identical.[5]

An agnostic would claim that "panis angelicus" is itself a figure, a symbol, and that Aquinas contradicts himself. But Aquinas would hold that there is no contradiction in the mystery of transubstantiation: the sentence is an act of faith, not an inadvertence. In other texts, Aquinas allows that the deficiencies of rational statement may be eked out, as in poetry, science, and theology, by recourse to metaphor and other figures.[6] None of these is adequate to articulate the divine mysteries, but they are helpful up to a point soon reached. These questions did not occur to us either in church or in school. In church we had our voices and the palpable eloquence of the Latin hymns, as irrefutable as the incense that often suffused them. In school we had the Christian Brothers' *Latin Grammar* at hand and, better still, our Latin teacher Mr. Crinion, who led us gracefully through an anthology of Virgil, Ovid, and Horace and a selection of Cicero's letters and speeches.

My affection for Latin pointed me toward those poems in our school anthology, *The Poet's Company,* that sounded Latin or were at least exotic in that way, resonant, unabashed, easy to memorize. Flecker's "The Old Ships" begins with feelings of expansiveness I wanted to have:

> I have seen old ships sail like swans asleep
> Beyond the village which men still call Tyre,
> With leaden age o'ercargoed, dipping deep

For Famagusta and the hidden sun
That rings black Cyprus with a lake of fire;
And all those ships were certainly so old
Who knows how oft with squat and noisy gun,
Questing brown slaves or Syrian oranges,
The pirate Genoese
Hell-raked them till they rolled
Blood, water, fruit and corpses up the hold.
But now through friendly seas they softly run,
Painted the mid-sea blue or shore-sea green,
Still patterned with the vine and grapes in gold.[7]

I don't recall being troubled by the indiscriminateness of the quests, "brown slaves" having much the same acoustic status as "Syrian oranges." So long as it sounded Latin, I recited it with the acoustic correlative of conviction. Another poem I memorized with the same ease was Masefield's "Cargoes," which begins with a full-throated stanza that includes one unforgettable line:

Quinquireme of Nineveh from distant Ophir,
Rowing home to haven in sunny Palestine,
With a cargo of ivory,
And apes and peacocks,
Sandalwood, cedarwood, and sweet white wine.[8]

I'm still not certain I know how to scan that last line.

If—to broach the unimaginable—I had been sent to a distinguished boarding school in Ireland or England, I might have felt something of what Neville felt, in Virginia Woolf's *The Waves*, on his first day at such a place:

A noble Roman air hangs over these austere quadrangles. Already the lights are lit in the form rooms. Those are laboratories perhaps; and that a library, where I shall explore the exactitude of the Latin language, and step firmly upon the well-laid sentences, and pronounce the explicit, the sonorous hexameters of Virgil, of Lucretius, and chant with a passion that is never obscure or formless the loves of Catullus, reading from a big book, a quarto with margins.[9]

It did not occur to me in Newry that I was in need of "a passion that is never obscure or formless." I was not aware of having any passions, except the one in favor of being alive. But otherwise Neville's sentiments were as distant from me as the moon: I could not have afforded them.

In due order—but with a delay of a year because of illness—I enrolled in the First Arts class at University College, Dublin, one of the constituent colleges of the National University of Ireland. At that time, to enter a college of the N.U.I., you had to have passed the senior leaving certificate examination in at least five subjects, including Latin, English, and Irish. Or you could take the matriculation examination of the N.U.I. on the same terms. Latin was obligatory, whatever qualifying examination you took. It was also my favorite subject. So I entered U.C.D. to read for a B.A. degree, taking as my first-year subjects Latin, English, Irish, history, and mathematics. I studied Latin with Professor Patrick Semple, who was approaching the end of his career, and Dr. John O'Meara, who was already on his way to becoming a major scholar of Augustine, Porphyry, and Eriugena. Professor Semple was too tired to entertain our questions. When someone asked him why Livy, reporting that some general had pitched his camp, sometimes wrote "castra posuit" and sometimes "posuit castra," he smiled the question aside. It hadn't yet struck me that Caesar always wrote "castra posuit," never "posuit castra" and that there might be some reason, unknown to me, for his postponing the subject of the sentence till the end, as in "Non respuit condicionem Caesar" in *De Bello Gallico*.[10] Dr. O'Meara was much more approachable than Professor Semple. He was evidently pleased to be asked to explain further the interrogative forms *ne, nonne,* and *utrum,* the difference between subjective and objective genitives, and why in Latin but not in English the main verb was so often held back to the end of the sentence. (Years later, I wondered to no purpose why T. S. Eliot, translating a line from Saint-Jean Perse's "Chanson"—"Il naissait un poulain sous les feuilles de bronze"—held back the verb till the end—"Under the bronze leaves a colt was foaled."[11]) Dr. O'Meara was also ready to respect my adolescent prejudice in thinking that Latin was more eloquent than English, and that the Latin factor accounted for whatever eloquence English could show.

Jeremiah J. Hogan was the professor of English and head of the department. In that capacity he prescribed the texts to be read, even those in Anglo-Saxon and Middle English and those in Anglo-Irish literature and drama, which were nominally in other hands. Professor Hogan thought that English literature in its supreme character was written in the period between the sixteenth and the nineteenth centuries: from Skelton to Newman and Hopkins, with Shakespeare and seventeenth century drama, poetry, and prose as the signal achievements. We might read the modern poets and novelists in our leisure hours, but they did not need to be taught. Nor were there any courses in American literature. I never heard Professor Hogan refer to an American book. He evidently shared the estimate of American literature that George Saintsbury entrusted to a footnote in his *History of English Prose Rhythm:*

> As I have mentioned Whitman, it may be asked
> why no other American prose-writers appear. Their

absence is not due to any incivility, and it is not wholly due to the desirableness of economising space. The reason is that, interesting as it might be to deal, say, with Emerson and Poe from our point of view, we should not find much, if anything, in them that gave us *new* observations. Emerson is practically represented by Carlyle; Poe at his best by De Quincey and even Landor; at his *not*-best by Charlotte Brontë. They have, as it were, their English "correspondents," and do business here by them.[12]

Once, when I spoke to Professor Hogan about T. S. Eliot, he said that he was an excellent prose writer.

Some years later, I met Professor Hogan walking along Earlsfort Terrace. He asked me whether I was happily settled in my post as an administrative officer in the Civil Service. When I told him that I did not regard myself as especially qualified for the Civil Service, he offered me a job as an assistant lecturer in his department. There was no mention of a vacancy, an advertisement, or a board of interview to report on the candidates. The job was mine if I wanted it. There was a mild question about my salary in the Civil Service. When I told him what it was, he remarked: "Oh, I think we can do somewhat better than that." The following morning, I submitted my resignation (in the first vernacular, Irish) to the minister for finance, giving him one month's notice. I took up my duties at U.C.D. in October, without any indication of the books I would be asked to teach. It emerged that Professor Hogan expected me and my few colleagues to teach, without discussion, whatever books he assigned to us. I gathered that he thought me reliable and competent to teach the books he found himself too busy to take on. He hoped to become dean of the Faculty of Arts, thereafter registrar, and finally president of the college, ambitions he realized in due time. Informally, I was thought to be his probable successor in the chair of English. So I taught the large classes and was assigned the most important works, the major Shakespearean tragedies with the exception of *King Lear,* which Professor Hogan reserved to himself. The only defect in my qualifications, I soon learned, was a precocious inclination to publish essays and eventually a book. Professor Hogan let me know, casually through my medievalist colleague T. P. Dunning, that he did not think young men should rush into print. He evidently worried that I might become my flaw. In other respects, I appeared to be sound.

Especially in one respect. Hogan—as I shall call him now that he is dead—was convinced that the glory of English literature consisted in its Latin relations. Shakespeare may have had little Latin and less Greek by comparison with Ben Jonson, but he had enough Latin to take possession of the Roman rhetorical tradition and to employ the full range of its figures. He saw the dramatic possibilities available in playing off the Latin against the Anglo-Saxon elements of English—as in Antony's dismembered speech to Eros late in the fourth act:

> Antony: Eros, thou yet behold'st me?
> Eros: Ay, noble lord.
> Antony: Sometime we see a cloud that's dragon-
>   ish;
>   A vapour sometime like a bear or lion,
>   A tower'd citadel, a pendent rock,
>   A forked mountain, or blue promontory
>   With trees upon 't, that nod unto the world,
>   And mock our eyes with air: thou hast seen
>   these signs;
>   They are black vesper's pageants.

Eros: Ay, my lord.
Antony: That which is now a horse, even with a
    thought
        The rack dislimns, and makes it indistinct,
        As water is in water.
Eros: It does, my lord.
Antony: My good knave Eros, now thy captain is
        Even such a body. (*Antony and Cleopatra,*
        4.14.1–13)[13]

It is the character of Latin, with Anglo-Saxon waiting to curb
its grandeurs, that makes this extraordinary moment possible.
Antony is at once dazed and idle, his occupation gone. As
Frank Kermode has noted, *rack* means drifting cloud, and *dis-limns* means what an artist doesn't do, the cloud—itself bro-ken—breaks the form instead of bringing it to definition.[14]
Here as elsewhere, Latin etymology sustains the high dream,
the visionary appearances good while they last. In *The Tempest*
we have the "cloud-capp'd towers, the gorgeous palaces,/The
solemn temples, the great globe itself . . . this insubstantial pag-eant." In *Macbeth:*

> Will all great Neptune's ocean wash this blood
> Clean from my hand? No, this my hand will rather
> The multitudinous seas incarnadine
> Making the green one red.
> *(2.2.60–63)*

In *Henry VIII* Wolsey says:

>   I shall fall
> Like a bright exhalation in the evening,
> And no man see me more.
> *(3.2.225–27)*

In *Antony and Cleopatra* the Latin of pendent rock, towered citadel, blue promontory, and black vesper's pageants keeps eloquence in play, however pathetically, till Antony turns to "my good knave Eros"—a stroke of theatrical genius—and brings the high talk to an end. The trees, like emperors, nod unto the world and mock our eyes with air: they are themselves the pageants so long as they hold their proclaimed form. But they, too, dissolve, leaving not a rack behind. Anglo-Saxon bears witness to their dissolution, "as water is in water."

I think the dramatic transitions from Latin to Anglo-Saxon alerted me to the force of transitions as such in poetry, sudden changes of vocabulary and tone: in Rilke's epitaph, "Rose, oh reiner Widerspruch, Lust," in James Wright's "Lying in a Hammock at William Duffy's Farm in Pine Island, Minnesota," the transition from "A chicken hawk floats over, looking for home" to "I have wasted my life." These are transitions without shown cause, their only reason is the character of the mind that ordains them. Expression is peremptory, it is its own reason.

I did not realize, teaching the syllabus as Professor Hogan prescribed it, that the quality common to the favored books was eloquence. His chosen writers were stylists, they had distinctive ways of moving among words. I never heard him discuss what made some books eloquent and some not. He did not comment on the political or ideological motives in literature. He respected the ideas that might be found in the vicinity of a book, but he was content to think of them as simply making a quiet context for it. How the ideas got into the book, and what happened when they entered, did not trouble him. He advised us to consult E. M. W. Tillyard's *The Elizabethan World Picture*, A. C. Bradley's *Shakespearean Tragedy*, and Basil Willey's *The Seventeenth Century Background*, but only for general instruction. The fact that the ideas elucidated in those books had turned into convictions for which people lived and died did not arise. Hogan was mainly interested in words, their origin, the company they kept, what it meant that one language was Celtic and another Indo-Germanic. His German, I heard, was just as accomplished as his English. But he drew a firm line around his references. He saw no reason why, talking about words, he should also be expected to discuss anything else. His wife regularly mentioned, on social occasions, that he intended writing a study of *King Lear:* it was, as she said, on the *tapis.* He gave a lecture to the Royal Irish Academy on the first scene of the play, but we heard nothing further of the book.

Meanwhile, he persisted in admiring Latin and the Latinical values in English. I once raised with him the necessity of providing courses, as I said, in "what the American universities call expository writing." He looked obscurely wounded at the mention of such a thing. Irish boys and girls who had passed through the secondary schools and taken their senior leaving certificate or matriculation examination were assumed to have acquired decent skill in reading and writing, grammar, punctuation, syntax, and rhetoric. As indeed most of them had. Besides, as Hogan remarked, the best way to learn to write good English was by reading good Latin. I agreed, having spent many congenial hours construing Virgil, Horace, Catullus, Livy, and Tacitus.

II

If I had thought of Latin as the privileged vehicle of civil discourse, and of eloquence as the common attribute of the syllabus I taught, I would not have been surprised by the persistence of Sir Thomas Browne's *Hydriotaphia: Urn-Burial* on the mandatory course for honours students. The presence of the other texts was self-explanatory, even Jonson's *Sejanus,* which

I could not warm to. But *Hydriotaphia* seemed an eccentric choice. No one to my knowledge was interested in the forty or fifty urns, Roman or more probably Saxon, found in a field near Norfolk in 1658. The meditation on death and funeral rites to which Browne ascends was remote from students and teachers alike: we were young, we knew we would never die. That left Browne's style, his zest in remembering Latin while writing in English. Most of *Hydriotaphia* seemed to me ridiculous, or quaint at best, but I find to this long day that certain passages of it have lodged in my mind and can be called up at will. "Some being of the opinion of *Thales,* that water was the originall of all things, thought it most equall to submit into the principle of putrefaction, and conclude in a moist relentment." The sentence is indeed most equal, a fine submission, with a gorgeous conclusion in a moist relentment:

> What Song the *Syrens* sang, or what name *Achilles*
> assumed when he hid himself among women,
> though puzzling Questions are not beyond all con-
> jecture. What time the persons of these Ossuaries
> entred the famous Nations of the dead, and slept
> with Princes and Counsellours, might admit a wide
> solution. But who were the proprietaries of these
> bones, or what bodies these ashes made up, were a
> question above Antiquarism. Not to be resolved by
> man, nor easily perhaps by spirits, except we consult
> the Provinciall Guardians, or tutelary Observators.
> Had they made as good provision for their names,
> as they have done for their Reliques, they had not
> so grossly erred in the art of perpetuation. But to
> subsist in bones, and be but Pyramidally extant, is
> a fallacy in duration. . . . And therefore restlesse
> inquietude for the diuturnity of our memories unto

present considerations, seems a vanity almost out of date, and superannuated peece of folly. We cannot hope to live so long in our names, as some have done in their persons, one face of *Janus* holds no proportion unto the other. 'Tis too late to be ambitious.[15]

It is typical of Browne, as if he learned from Shakespeare the drama of transitions, to begin a sentence with a flourish of the main theme—what song the Syrens sang or what name Achilles assumed—then to draw into its ambit a subordinate clause or two, and have the sentence subside in a dying cadence—"are not beyond all conjecture," "might admit a wide solution," "were a question above Antiquarism," and in other places "we have no authentic conjecture," "is not absurdly doubted," and "'twere a query too sad to insist on." He had many ways of saying that he didn't know the answer, and of being sanguine in the confession of ignorance. Ultimately, the questions would be resolved, he seemed to think, but not by him. Walter Pater thought Browne's terminations were such that busy posterity would abbreviate them—forgetting that his own were also in danger of the shears—but there is no sign of that. There is more merit in Pater's complaint—made with pith unusual for him—that Browne's meditations are "too like a lifetime following of one's own funeral."[16] Meanwhile Browne savored the syllables of his Latin—*perpetuation, duration, diuturnity, superannuated*—and enjoyed the eloquence of his aphorisms—"Life is a pure flame, and we live by an invisible Sun within us"—his rhetorical questions and *exempla:*

> To be namelesse in worthy deeds exceeds an infamous history. The *Canaanitish* woman lives more happily without a name, than *Herodias* with one.

And who had not rather have been the good thief, then *Pilate?*

But the iniquity of oblivion blindely scatter-eth her poppy, and deals with the memory of men without distinction to merit of perpetuity. Who can but pity the founder of the Pyramids? *Hero-stratus* lives that burnt the Temple of *Diana,* he is almost lost that built it; Time hath spared the Epi-taph of *Adrians* horse, confounded that of himself. In vain we compute our felicities by the advantage of our good names, since bad have equall durations; and *Thersites* is like to live as long as *Agamemnon.* Who knows whether the best of men be known? or whether there be not more remarkable persons for-got, then any that stand remembred in the known account of time? without the favour of the everlast-ing Register the first man had been as unknown as the last, and *Methuselahs* long life had been his only Chronicle.[17]

This kind of writing is sustained, if not by the wisdom of the ages, then by that of the Latin centuries. Browne's style is En-glish in its syntax, Latin in its diction.[18] In his essay "Of Lan-guages," he composed six passages of modern English and set beside each his translation of it into "Saxon," as he called it, to prove that while "from the French we have borrowed many Substantives, Adjectives and some Verbs," still "the great Body of Numerals, auxiliary Verbs, Articles, Pronouns, Adverbs, Conjunctions and Prepositions, which are the distinguishing and lasting part of a Language, remain with us from the Saxon, which, having suffered no great alteration for many hundred years, may probably still remain, though the English swell with the inmates of Italian, French and Latin."[19] He made his own contribution to the Latin swelling, mainly because of his pre-occupation with deaths and dyings. The Latin element in the passage I've quoted from *Hydriotaphia* has mortality in every word: *iniquity, oblivion, perpetuity, felicities, durations,* the whole empire of things acknowledged along with their fated disappearance. It is because Latin has resources beyond local expression or discursive need that we retain Latin words—*copia* and *cursus*—for their plenitude. The only comment I recall Professor Hogan making about Browne's style in *Hydriotaphia* was that he was occasionally imperfect in allowing a line of verse to invade his prose: "Darkness and light divide the course of time" was a perfect line of iambic pentameter, with the substitution of a trochee for an iamb in the first foot. Anglo-Saxon prose had many such lines, Hogan noted, but they were no longer approved.

When it fell to me to teach *Hydriotaphia,* I concealed my misgiving by reading most of the fifth chapter aloud in class, and referring to selected passages from Browne's *Religio Medici* and *The Garden of Cyrus* to extend the context of allusion. I also read some sentences from Johnson's *Life* of Browne, those in which Johnson, a critic who rarely felt the need of second thoughts, qualified his disapproval of Browne's style by adverting to the merits that accompanied its defects. He began by thinking it perverse:

> To have great excellencies, and great faults, "magnae virtutes nec minora vitia, is the poesy," says our author, "of the best natures." This poesy may be properly applied to the style of Browne: It is vigorous, but rugged; it is learned, but pedantick; it is deep, but obscure; it strikes, but does not please; it commands, but does not allure: his tropes are harsh, and his combinations uncouth. He fell into an age,

in which our language began to lose the stability which it had obtained in the time of Elizabeth; and was considered by every writer as a subject on which he might try his plastick skill, by moulding it according to his own fancy.

Milton took the first liberty, and Browne seconded him:

> Milton, in consequence of this encroaching licence, began to introduce the Latin idiom: and Browne, though he gave less disturbance to our structures and phraseology, yet poured in a multitude of exotick words; many, indeed, useful and significant, which, if rejected, must be supplied by circumlocution, such as *commensality* for the state of many living at the same table; but many superfluous, as a *paralogical* for an unreasonable doubt; and some so obscure, that they conceal his meaning rather than explain it, as *arthritical analogies* for parts that serve some animals in the place of joints.

At this point Johnson begins to think of Browne as a metaphysical poet, like Donne and his school in whose poems, according to Johnson's *Life* of Cowley, "the most heterogeneous ideas are yoked by violence together."[20] Browne's style "is, indeed, a tissue of many languages; a mixture of heterogeneous words, brought together from distant regions, with terms originally appropriated to one art, and drawn by violence into the service of another." But Johnson concedes that there is another side to the account:

> He must, however, be confessed to have augmented our philosophical diction; and in defence of his uncommon words and expressions, we must consider, that he had uncommon sentiments, and was

not content to express in many words that idea for which any language could supply a single term.

But his innovations are sometimes pleasing, and his temerities happy: he has many "verba ardentia," forcible expressions, which he would never have found, but by venturing to the utmost verge of propriety; and flights which would never have been reached, but by one who had very little fear of the shame of falling.[21]

These passages in Johnson provided me with enough critical and terminological niceties to keep me audible, if not eloquent, on *Hydriotaphia* for the requisite number of classes.

III

The question of terminology was a consideration, though not yet a problem. Professor Hogan's syllabus did not include any courses in literary theory or the history of literary criticism. We were expected to know what we were doing, without troubling ourselves about the theory of it. There were a few prescribed texts of obvious theoretical bearing: Aristotle's *Poetics*, Wordsworth's preface to the second edition of *Lyrical Ballads* (1800), Coleridge's *Biographia Literaria*, Newman's *Idea of a University*, and Arnold's *On Translating Homer*. Coleridge's definition of a poem was enough to begin with:

A poem is that species of composition, which is opposed to works of science, by proposing for its *immediate* object pleasure, not truth; and from all other species (having *this* object in common with it) it is discriminated by proposing to itself such delight from the *whole*, as is compatible with a distinct gratification from each component *part*.[22]

That was clear, if not clear enough for young minds. We added this passage from Wordsworth:

> If I had undertaken a systematic defence of the theory upon which these poems are written, it would have been my duty to develop the various causes upon which the pleasure received from metrical language depends. Among the chief of these causes is to be reckoned a principle which must be well known to those who have made any of the Arts the object of accurate reflection; I mean the pleasure which the mind derives from the perception of similitude in dissimilitude. This pleasure is the great spring of the activity of our minds and their chief feeder. From this principle the direction of the sexual appetite, and all the passions connected with it take their origin: It is the life of our ordinary conversation; and upon the accuracy with which similitude in dissimilitude, and dissimilitude in similitude are perceived, depend our taste and our moral feelings.[23]

Aristotle suggested a mainly "dramatistic" emphasis, leading to notions of action, motive, role playing, and coherence of characters and plot. Arnold extended one's vocabulary, enabling one to recognize *rapidity* of style and so forth, but mostly showing what it was like to engage in a literary argument—a question of style—that was also an acute cultural and social issue. But with Coleridge and Wordsworth in our minds, we were not prepared to find in literature and literary criticism a site of trouble, such as that described by John Guillory three or four years ago:

> I do agree that literary criticism is a curiously troubled discipline today, and that part of its

trouble is directly related to the ambivalence that academic literary critics seem to express toward the object of their discipline. This ambivalence typically takes two forms: first, the disinclination to regard works of literature as the necessary or constitutive object of literary criticism, and second, an even stronger aversion to a way of talking about literature in which the pleasure of the literary work is acknowledged as its chief reason for being, and correlatively that the communication of that pleasure to the readers of criticism is at least one of the purposes of criticism.

Guillory went on to say that the "turn to the political" in literary criticism is one way that critics have of "doing what they have always done, which is to neutralize pleasure on behalf of more socially acceptable—or as the case may be, more socially transgressive—agendas."[24] In Dublin we were not aware of such agendas.

Style was the only consideration: it testified to an individual writer's way of being alive in the language. Stevens calls it "the imagination's Latin"—

He tries by a peculiar speech to speak

The peculiar potency of the general,
To compound the imagination's Latin with
The lingua franca et jocundissima[25]

—while he gives the vernacular, too, in Latin. Style: I call it eloquence, if only to separate its words from those we use—or others use—in talking about the styles of women, this season's fashions, Frank Gehry's museum in Bilbao, Roger Federer's tennis, Astaire's dancing, Fischer-Dieskau's *lieder*, Daniel Webster's oratory, someone's way of walking along the street. Eloquence is akin to style, except that it is a narrower consideration, literary rather than in a wider sense cultural. Sainte-Beuve said of the author of *Madame Bovary:* "A precious quality distinguishes M. Gustave Flaubert from other more or less exact observers, who, these days, pride themselves on faithfully rendering reality, and sometimes succeed at it: he has style."[26] There is a further consideration: if you have style, you do well to have several styles, as Browne has.

In Dublin, I thought a good deal about style and eloquence. I was a student of *lieder* at the Royal Irish Academy of Music, where I strengthened my conviction that formal eloquence was the only good reason for the existence of music. The production of "virtual time"—in Susanne Langer's formulation—was the only theory of music I found convincing. I had forgotten, though I had read it several times, the passage in *Counter-Statement* where Kenneth Burke says that "art, at least in the great periods when it has flowered, was the conversion, or transcendence, of emotion into eloquence, and was thus a factor added to life."[27] Better conversion than transcendence, because it keeps the action on the ground: it is a program large enough for my needs. If eloquence is a factor added to life, what it mainly says is that nothing necessarily coincides with itself: in passing from existence to expression, there is always the possibility of enhancement. Positivism is a tedious lie. It may be true, as Stevens says in "The Comedian as the Letter C," that "The words of things entangle and confuse. / The plum survives its poems."[28] But the plum does not survive by being returned to mere being, as if released from the words of it and cleansed of their eloquence. Against Stevens for the moment I cite Diderot: "The word is not the thing, but a flash in the light of which one perceives it."[29]

How to distinguish eloquence from its strutting cousins—grandiloquence, magniloquence, bombast, cant? Only in particulars. Marianne Moore quoted the Apostle James—"For the sun is no sooner risen with a burning heat, but it witherith the grass, and the flower thereof falleth, and the grace of the fashion of it perisheth: so always shall the rich man fade away in his ways." Moore said: "Substitute 'the grace of its fashion perisheth' and overconscious correctness is weaker than the actual version, in which eloquence escapes grandiloquence by virtue of gusto."[30] Moore also writes, in the poem "Silence," of superior people, that they "can be robbed of speech / by speech which has delighted them."[31] In "The Equilibrists" John Crowe Ransom escapes grandiloquence while moving from the word *period* to its near-synonym the Latinical *saeculum* in the next line, because *saeculum* is immediately attended by *Death*, a theme on which Latin can claim to be expert: "A kinder saeculum begins with Death." Two stanzas later he brings the reverberant Latin to an end with a strict vernacular:

> Great lovers lie in Hell, the stubborn ones
> Infatuate of the flesh upon the bones;
> Stuprate, they rend each other when they kiss,
> The pieces kiss again, no end to this.[32]

I had to consult the Latin dictionary to find that *stuprate* is from *stuprare*, to defile, *stuprum*, pollution by lust, a debauching, ravishing violation. No such recourse was necessary to deal with the Latin of the first line of Ransom's "Dead Boy": "The little cousin is dead, by foul subtraction."[33] In arithmetic I was already familiar with the Latinical subtraction, addition, and multiplication.

But I should not imply that my sense of Latin was at all *comprehensive*. How could it be, lacking Greek? I acquired some competence in classical Latin and the ecclesiastical Latin of the hymns and the Mass, but I had only a vague understanding of the *romanitas* that E. R. Curtius clarifies in *European Literature and the Latin Middle Ages* or of the later fortune of Latin as it is expounded in Erich Auerbach's *Literary Language and Its Public in Late Antiquity and in the Middle Ages.* "Had we but world enough and time . . ."

Some years ago I thought of compiling an anthology, a commonplace book, in which every chosen item would drive readers into an *altitudo* of pleasure—to think that there could be such eloquence, sentences, cadences, in what seems otherwise an ordinary world. Like Professor Hogan's study of *King Lear,* it has been on my *tapis,* a book I cherish if only because I have not written it. Some of the items I quote with delight in the present book would have found a place in that one.

3

Song Without Words

We normally advert to eloquence when we note the exuberance with which a word, a phrase, a sentence, or a line of verse presents itself as if it had broken free from its setting and declared its independence. This explains why we remember a certain eloquent moment and, a split second or an hour later, or never, the context in which it appeared. A selection from my own failing memory: "She should have died hereafter." ". . . the seal's wide spindrift gaze toward paradise." "The troubled midnight and the noon's repose." "In the mountains, there you feel free." "Cover her face; mine eyes dazzle; she died young." "And sweet reluctant amorous delay." "J'ai tout lu, se disait-elle." "I coulda bin a contender." "You talkin' to me?" "Blown hair is sweet, brown hair over the mouth blown." "agnosco veteris vestigia flammae." "So have I heard and do in part believe it." "And my poor fool is hanged!" "Those are pearls that were his eyes." "Thou are indeed just, Lord, if I contend with thee." "The fire that stirs about her when she stirs." "Inns are not residences." "But the snows and summer grieve and dream." "A bracelet of bright hair about the bone." "Did he who made the Lamb make thee?" "Twice no one dies." "On his wise shoulders through the checkerwork of leaves the sun flung spangles, dancing coins." "Dear incomprehension, it's thanks to you I'll be myself, in the end."

What these have in common in my mind is their irreducibility: each has a context which in some cases I have forgotten, but each seems to be surrounded by empty space. Each exists in an eternal present moment. And each is so independent in that moment that it doesn't need to declare its independence. When one or another of these items comes to my mind, it makes me feel that nothing else in the whole world matters; that this is what life amounts to. The narrator in Blanchot's *L'Arrêt de mort* says:

> Je parle de faits qui semblent infimes et je laisse de cöté les événements publics. Ces événements ont été très grands et ils m'ont occupé tous les jours. Mais, aujourd'hui, ils pourrissent, leur histoire est morte et mortes aussi ces heures et cette vie qui alors ont été les miennes. Ce qui parle, c'est la minute présente et celle qui va la suivre. A tous ceux qu'elle abrite, l'ombre du monde d'hier plait encore, mais elle sera effacée.[1]

In Lydia Davis's translation:

> I am talking about things that seem negligible, and I am ignoring public events. These events were very important and they occupied my attention all the time. But now they are rotting away, their story is dead, and the hours and the life that were then mine are dead too. What is eloquent is the passing moment and the moment that will come after it. The shadow of yesterday's world is still pleasant for people who take refuge in it, but it will fade.[2]

II

In "The Second Coming," Yeats tries to conceive an image of the impending historical dispensation, as he takes it for granted dreadfully but also with the force of desire for it, an image antithetical to that of the Christ child born two thousand years ago. What occurs to him is "a shape with lion body and the head of a man," "moving its slow thighs," "while all about it / Reel shadows of the indignant desert birds."[3] Not birds but their shadows, the only parts of them that cannot escape from the weird shape in the sand. The eloquence of the passage breaks forth in *indignant*. It is astonishing that the birds should be thought to feel what we would feel, faced with a new, wild image that would govern our lives. *Reel:* to stagger or whirl, as here probably to whirl in circles, the birds being unable to release themselves from the appalling image below them in the desert. *Indignant* in this poem is the word I think of when I reflect on the distinctive quality of Yeats's eloquence, though there are other poems and other words in which his imagination is more cryptic or more esoteric.

There is no reason to claim that *indignant* in this poem, thrilling as it strikes me as being, will be deemed eloquent by every reader and for all literate time. If the word, the line, and the poem are—to use a criterion of Whitehead's, "patient of interpretation in terms of Laws which happen to interest us"— there is a good chance of their appearing eloquent for some time to come.[4] But if a cultural change should occur, such that indignation would be held to be a childish or otherwise trivial emotion in any and all circumstances, Yeats's *indignant* would lose its force and be diminished not necessarily in the light of eternity but in a more topical light. We must stop short of trying to define eloquence once for all, mainly for Nietzsche's reason, that "only something that has no history can be defined."[5] Meanwhile—to curb the speculation and keep to tangible issues—*indignant* seems to declare its independence, but it doesn't, it remains loyally if not unquestioningly within the syntax of its sentence. There is no sign in it of that irritable gesturing with which many modern writers indicate their dissatisfaction with language, their feeling that even if there are plenty of words, they are not the right ones for their purposes. Workers in other arts don't seem to feel this. Composers are never heard complaining that they lack the right notes or that the range of tones, semitones, and quarter tones is not enough; painters, that paint and canvas are intolerably restricting; sculptors, that the materials at their disposal are spiritually crude; architects, that stone, iron, glass, and wood are limited vehicles; film directors, that the camera is a rough instrument. But writers are constantly complaining about their means; like Eliot's Sweeney saying "But I've gotta use words when I talk to you." They seem to yearn to have a different kind of genius and a different instrument. I'm not thinking of *Finnegans Wake*. That book gives an impression of having been written because Joyce intuited with delight a linguistic possibility, not because he found the words he used in *Dubliners, A Portrait of the Artist as a Young Man*, and the first half of *Ulysses* inadequate. Eliot is a better example of the yearning for a different vocation. He often writes as if he wanted to be a composer, or if not that, to live in the hinterland between poetry and music. When he invokes "the auditory imagination," in *The Use of Poetry and the Use of Criticism*, he sounds as if he wanted to distract words from their mere reference and dissociate them into free syllables and assonances. Walter Pater tempted writers toward this yearning when, for an apparently good reason, he presented music as the ideally consummate art:

> *All art constantly aspires towards the condition of music.* For while in all other kinds of art it is possible to distinguish the matter from the form, and the understanding can always make this distinction, yet it is the constant effort of art to obliterate

it. That the mere matter of a poem, for instance, its subject, namely, its given incidents or situation — that the mere matter of a picture, the actual circumstances of an event, the actual topography of a language — should be nothing without the form, the spirit, of the handling, that this form, this mode of handling, should become an end in itself, should penetrate every part of the matter: this is what all art constantly strives after, and achieves in different degrees.

Art, according to Pater, "is thus always striving to be independent of the mere intelligence, to become a matter of pure perception, to get rid of its responsibilities to its subject or material."[6]

Music may have been the preeminent art, but there was also the dance, regarded by some masters — Mallarmé, Yeats, Valéry — as the supreme song without words. Geoffrey Hill has protested against this impulse as an extravagance. When writers aspire toward the condition of music or the even more occult state of silence ("Words, after speech, reach / Into the silence") they yield to "angelism," as Maritain called it, the "refusal of the creature to submit to or be ruled by any of the exigencies of the created natural order."[7] They want to be angels, free of earth, its knowledge and its means. Allen Tate thought that Poe was the supreme exemplar of this refusal. Hill comments:

> In the essay "Poetry and Drama" Eliot speaks of "a fringe of indefinite extent, of feeling which we can only detect, so to speak, out of the corner of the eye and can never completely focus. . . . At such moments, we touch the border of these feelings which only music can express." As Eliot well knew,

however, a poet must also turn back, with whatever weariness, disgust, love barely distinguishable from hate, to confront "the indefinite extent" of language itself and seek his "focus" there. In certain contexts the expansive, outward gesture towards the condition of music is a helpless gesture of surrender, oddly analogous to that stylish aesthetic of despair, that desire for the ultimate integrity of silence, to which so much eloquence has been so frequently and indefatigably devoted.[8]

Hill qualifies his rebuke with "also" and "in certain contexts," but his large argument is not decisive. Poets do what they can; there is no merit in declaring what they "must" do. Eliot is among those poets who discover their creative power in the incantatory capacities of language rather than in the semantic responsibility of words and sentences. He seems to be immersed in the language before any referential or discursive need of it arises. He has more in common with Poe, Pater, and Swinburne than he cares to acknowledge. Instances of his eloquence seem to break forth before he has accepted the responsibility of attending to local meanings: later—especially in the poems from "Ash Wednesday" to *Four Quartets*—he attended to them dutifully enough and made peace with their requirements, subject to the imperative of his genius.

But there are other forms of eloquence, at the opposite extreme from incantation or "the sublime," which seem to derive their poetic power from gestures and actions imagined as prior to language or aside from it. These cannot be "songs without words," since they are in language, but they gain their impetus from the apprehension of things in the world that are not—or not yet—verbal. When we remember them, we recall what is done, and only later what is said on their occasions. In *Blood*

Meridian, after many pages of mayhem, the judge goes down to the outhouse. The boy opens the door:

> The judge was seated upon the closet. He was naked and he rose up smiling and gathered him in his arms against his immense and terrible flesh and shot the wooden barlatch home behind him.

What happens then, we have no way of knowing. Two men from the bar come down to the jakes. One of them opens the door:

> Good God almighty, he said.
> What is it?
> He didn't answer. He stepped past the other and went back up the walk. The other man stood looking after him. Then he opened the door and looked in.[9]

What he saw, we will never know. But after three hundred pages of American gothic, the laconic ending is unforgettable, its eloquence is so nearly without words. Whatever images we resort to, we take up on our own responsibility. McCarthy doesn't say a helpful word. Even in such a voluble book as *Moby-Dick,* we remember not the great speeches—not even Father Mapple's sermon—but episodes, Ahab's nailing the doubloon to the masthead, Queequeg in his coffin, Ishmael finding Queequeg in bed beside him, Ahab refusing to help the captain of the *Rachel,* Pip in Ahab's cabin. If I recall Ahab's soliloquy in his cabin, what I recall is that it took place, not the gorgeous language that begins—I transcribe it from chapter 37—"I leave a white and turbid wake; pale waters, paler cheeks, where'er I sail."[10]

Why talk or write of eloquence, then, if you can find instances of it nearly anywhere between silence and grand opera?

Or even in the silences that punctuate the arias? It is to throw a coloring of particular interests and expectations over a field of expression; to stake a claim apart from the more insistent claims of economics and politics; to turn aside from war. And for Blanchot's reason, quoted a few pages back: "Ce qui parle, c'est la minute présente et celle qui va la suivre." The considerations that point to eloquence—and point it up—are not historical. When we bring forward instances of it, we invoke them as if their being historical didn't matter; they are here and now and for the moment in which we appreciate them. It is as if they were removed from time, if only for as long as our attention lasts.

<h1 style="text-align:center">III</h1>

A prime instance of a song without words is the knocking on the gate in *Macbeth*. The scene is Macbeth's castle in Inverness. King Duncan and his retinue have arrived to celebrate the defeat of the Norwegians, the execution of the rebellious Thane of Cawdor, and the promotion of Macbeth to Cawdor's title. The royal party is to lodge for the night in the castle and to enjoy the hospitality appropriate to the occasion. The Weird Sisters have put into Macbeth's mind the image of himself as Thane of Cawdor, and ultimately as king. The first part of their prophecy has come about, so there is a strong presumption in favor of the second. Macbeth and Lady Macbeth have already talked over their possibly killing Duncan, despite his many virtues and the obligations of service they have to a king. Awaiting her husband, Lady Macbeth drives herself into further extremes of resolve and ferocity. Macbeth hangs back a little, talks of calling off the assassination, and rehearses the many reasons against killing the king. But Lady Macbeth goads him into it and lays out the plan. Duncan will be asleep, and Lady Macbeth will ply his two chamberlains with enough drink to annul their memories and their minds. A bell rings: Macbeth interprets it as a summons to do the deed.

In the next scene, Lady Macbeth is alone, having sent the grooms into a drunken stupor. There is a sound:

> Hark! Peace!
> It was the owl that shriek'd, the fatal bellman,
> Which gives the sterns't good-night.

Macbeth enters:

> I have done the deed.

But he talks brainsick stuff about noises and nightmares. Besides, he has neglected to leave the daggers in the king's chamber, and Lady Macbeth orders him to go back and smear the grooms with blood. He can't; she must do it herself. She leaves, and there is a knock. Lady Macbeth returns, having bloodied the faces of the grooms. There is another knock "at the south entry." "Retire we to our chamber," Lady Macbeth says. And immediately there is another knock, whereupon she tells Macbeth to put on his dressing gown, "lest occasion call us, and show us to be watchers." "To know my deed, 'twere best not know myself," Macbeth says, and there is another knock. "Wake Duncan with thy knocking! I would thou couldst!" he says, and they both leave the scene.

The knocking continues, and this time the porter, somewhat the worse for drink, makes his slow way to the gate:

> Here's a knocking indeed! If a man were porter
> of hell-gate, he should have old turning the key.
> (Knock.) Knock, knock, knock! Who's there, i' the
> name of Beelzebub? Here's a farmer, that hanged
> himself on the expectation of plenty: come in time;

have napkins enow about you; here you'll sweat for't. *(Knock.)* Knock, knock! Who's there, in the other devil's name? Faith, here's an equivocator, that could swear in both the scales against either scale; who committed treason enough for God's sake, yet could not equivocate to heaven: O, come in, equivocator. *(Knock.)* Knock, knock, knock! Faith, here's an English tailor come hither, for stealing out of a French hose: come in, tailor; here you may roast your goose. *(Knock.)* Knock, knock; never at quiet! What are you? But this place is too cold for hell. I'll devil-porter it no further: I had thought to have let in some of all professions that goes the primrose way to the everlasting bonfire. *(Knock.)* Anon, anon! I pray you remember the porter. (2.3.1–26)

Then he opens the gate to Macduff and Lennox, who have come to see Macbeth. The porter talks to them about drink that leads a man toward sex but makes him incapable of the performance, "equivocates him in a sleep, and, giving him the lie, leaves him" (2.3.40).

Coleridge thought the Porter scene so "low" and "disgusting" that he refused to believe it was Shakespeare's work:

> This low porter soliloquy I believe written for the mob by some other hand, perhaps with Shake-speare's consent—and that finding it take, he with the remaining ink of a pen otherwise employed just interpolated it with the sentence, "I'll devil-porter it no further" and what follows to "bonfire." Of the rest not one syllable has the ever-present being of Shakespeare.[11]

Coleridge was right in one respect, that the whole episode (including the knocking that frightened Macbeth and his wife) was written not only for the mob but for the mob in each of us. We have had a scene of horror and murder, not at all alleviated by the domestic crisis between Macbeth and Lady Macbeth. The murder is committed offstage, but we hear enough of the machinery of it, with talk of knives, the sodden grooms, the second visit to smear their faces, the nightmares, enough to leave us wanting some relief from blood. The eloquence of the episode depends on the dramatist's lowering the emotional temperature, getting rid of the two murderers for a while, bringing forward a low-level comedian to deal with the knocking at the gate that still persists, and yet keeping one of the images—the murder scene as hell, as the gate is the gate to it—still in play, if at the lowest level of intensity. What is appeased is—as Kenneth Burke would say—the psychology of the audience. It does not take much skill—and very little verbal finesse—to effect such a transition. High brows and low brows are at least occasionally at one by virtue of the biological level on which they live.

De Quincey gives a more elaborate account of this sequence in *Macbeth,* but not a contradictory one:

> Here, as I have said, the retiring of the human heart and the entrance of the fiendish heart was to be expressed and made sensible. Another world has stept in; and the murderers are taken out of the region of human things, human purposes, human desires. They are transfigured: Lady Macbeth is "unsexed"; Macbeth has forgot that he was born of woman; both are conformed to the image of devils; and the world of devils is suddenly revealed. But how shall this be conveyed and made palpable? In order that

a new world may step in, this world must for a time disappear. The murderers and the murder must be insulated—cut off by an immeasurable gulf from the ordinary tide and succession of human affairs—locked up and sequestered in some deep recess; we must be made sensible that the world of ordinary life is suddenly arrested, laid asleep, tranced, racked into a dread armistice; time must be annihilated, relation to things without abolished; and all must pass self-withdrawn into a deep syncope and suspension of earthly passion. Hence it is that, when the deed is done, when the work of darkness is perfect, then the world of darkness passes away like a pageantry in the clouds; the knocking at the gate is heard, and it makes known audibly that the reaction has commenced: the human has made its reflux upon the fiendish; the pulses of life are beginning to beat again; and the re-establishment of the goings-on of the world in which we live first makes us profoundly sensible of the awful parenthesis that had suspended them.[12]

It is a temporary release, effected by the simplest means—a few knocks on the gate, a rigmarole that passes for comedy. Nearly any words would have done as well. The eloquence is the *sprezzatura* of sequence, one set of images leading to another not for logical but for rhetorical reasons, till these in turn are replaced by the next phase of murder. The knocking on the gate is rudimentary eloquence, but it is enough to keep an interval between one phase of horror and the next, when Macduff discovers the murder, Macbeth kills the grooms, Duncan's horses go mad and eat each other, Macbeth has Banquo murdered, Lady Macbeth goes mad and kills herself, and in the end Macduff beheads

Macbeth, and Malcolm, Duncan's son, takes up the throne of Scotland. The eloquence of the knocking on the gate is finesse of sequence, verbal in the most perfunctory sense.

IV

Madame Bovary is rich in songs without words. I'll mention two of them. Charles Bovary, the local doctor, recently become a widower, makes several house calls to Les Bertaux, home of old Rouault, a farmer who has broken his leg. Rouault is looked after by his daughter Emma:

> As was the custom in the country, [Emma] offered [the doctor] something to drink. He refused, but she insisted, and finally asked him, with a laugh, to join her in a glass of liqueur. So she fetched a bottle of curaçao from the cupboard, reached down two tiny glasses, filled one to the brim, poured just a drop into the other and then, after clinking glasses with him, raised it to her mouth. As it was almost empty, she leaned right back to drink and, with her head tilted, her lips pushed forward and her neck taut, she laughed at finding nothing, while the tip of her tongue, poking between her beautiful teeth, delicately licked at the bottom of the glass.
>
> She sat down and resumed her work, a white cotton stocking she was darning; she sat with her head bent over it, not speaking. Charles did not speak either. A draught of air from under the door stirred a little dust on the flagstones; he watched it slowly move, hearing only the pounding inside his head and the distant cry of a laying hen in the yard. From time to time Emma would freshen her cheeks with

her palms, which she then cooled on the knobs of the huge iron firedogs.[13]

The erotic force of this episode is entirely the result of act and gesture; it has as little to do with words as is consistent with the minimally verbal character of writing. Emma's laugh, before the drink and again while trying to drink the drop at the bottom of the glass ("et enfin lui offrit, en riant, de prendre un verre de liqueur avec elle" and later, "Comme il était presque vide, elle se renversait pour boire: et, la tête en arrière, les lèvres avancées, le cou tendu, elle riait de ne rien sentir, tandis que le bout de sa langue, passant entre ses dents fines, léchait à petits coups le fond du verre") is a silent promise of happiness.[14] Her licking up the drop of curaçao—lips, tongue, and laughter—is an erotic ritual, not a symbol of pleasure but itself the pleasure. Not a word is spoken—we're not told her words of invitation or the doctor's of refusal. The refusal doesn't matter, she gets the glasses anyway, and the liqueur. It's as if Flaubert had only to imagine a woman doing such a thing, and its consequences. He didn't need to think of a conversation going on. We hear not a word from Charles, only the pounding inside his head ("et il entendait seulement le battement intérieur de sa tête") and the noise of a hen, far off in the yard, laying an egg. Emma's further "business" with her cheeks, the palms of her hands, and the knobs of the firedogs ("sur la pomme de fer des grands chenets") is erotic because every detail of her movements has always been warmed at the erotic flame.

Flaubert's eloquence in this passage is an achievement of form and impartiality: it doesn't depend on raising the verbal stakes or thinking of the higher possibilities of style. The distinctiveness of the passage is that it pays no attention to distinctiveness; it holds its own measure, and regards—or pretends to regard—one item of behavior as on the same level as another.

It is the character of his aesthetic sense in *Madame Bovary* to maintain from his subject matter the same aversive distance, with occasional slight concessions to imply that, say, Emma's feeling are not always as trivial as they appear: there may be something, a little, to be said for them.

Toward the end of September, Emma (now married to Charles Bovary and the restlessness of ennui) is invited to La Vaubyessard, home of the Marquis d'Andervilliers. Dr. Bovary has cured an abscess in the marquis's mouth by a simple lancing. The marquis's steward, sent to pay the bill, noticed that there were some splendid cherries in the doctor's modest garden. The marquis, whose own cherries were not thriving, asked the doctor for a few grafts, which Charles was honored to provide. Making a point of thanking Charles personally, the marquis saw Emma, noted her pretty figure and her stylish manner of address. It was then decided, at the château, that an invitation to the young couple would not be beyond the limit of social condescension. Monsieur and Madame Bovary set out in their gig, with a large trunk tied on behind and a hatbox in front. Emma is escorted into the château by the marquis. We read of the château, the portrait gallery, the billiard room, the guests, the servants, the dinner served, the marquis's father-in-law dribbling his soup, the ballroom, the music, the first dance, the overheard conversations. Charles is present, but Emma has forbidden him to dance. She herself dances with several gentlemen, one of them a viscount, but Charles leans against a door and gradually falls asleep until it is time for him to go to bed:

> The ballroom was stifling; the lamps were growing dim. People were moving out into the billiard room. A servant climbed onto a chair and broke a couple of panes; at the sound of the shattering glass, Madame Bovary looked round and saw, in

the garden, pressed against the window panes, the faces of peasants, staring in.[15]

The eloquence of this episode is entirely social and cultural. We are mainly told of the reasons that are not given. "L'air du bal était lourd." To whom? No one complained, or if they did, the complaint is not recorded. The servant ("Un domestique") has not been instructed by the marquise to let in some air. He has not sought permission to climb a chair and break two windows for that purpose—which presumably will have to be repaired tomorrow. Emma, to whom much of high life is new—she has never seen a pomegranate before or tasted a pineapple—knows enough to know that whatever a servant does in a marquis's château is proper. The little incident is eloquent to the extent to which its social codes are complete: the niceties of class have been maintained, the extravagance, the waste. The picture is culturally replete, all the spaces have been filled in.

When she sees the faces of the peasants looking through the broken windows, Emma withdraws into an entirely egotistical reverie:

> Suddenly she thought of Les Bertaux. She saw the farm, the muddy pond, her father in his smock under the apple trees, and she saw herself in earlier days, skimming cream with her finger from the earthenware milk pans in the dairy. But, in the dazzling splendors of the present moment, her past life, always until then so vivid, was vanishing completely, and she almost doubted that she had ever lived it. Here she was, at the ball; beyond it, now, everything else was veiled in shadow. Here she was eating a maraschino ice, holding in her left hand the scalloped silver-gilt saucer, her eyes half-closed, the spoon between her teeth.[16]

Emma is not stupid, though Flaubert often gives us reason to think that she might be. But it is typical of her consciousness that whatever she directs it upon immediately starts fading under her attention. The quality of her memory is such that nothing survives it, the effect is always the evanescence of the object. She pays attention, then she doubts the reality or the worth of the object of it, and lets it lapse. Flaubert makes repetition do the work of displacement: one "Elle" leads only to another:

> Elle était là; puis, autour du bal, il n'y avait plus que de l'ombre, étalée sur tout le reste. Elle mangeait alors une glace au marasquin, qu'elle tenait de la main gauche dans une coquille de vermeil, et fermait à demi les yeux, la cuiller entre les dents.[17]

It is also typical of Flaubert's eloquence—which talk of his irony often suppresses—that his notations are disinterested, each of them allowed to have whatever value we are willing to give it; he has not enforced a negative implication as relentlessly as we might expect. Margaret Mauldon's translation is a little heavy at this point: "in the dazzling splendors of the present moment" is more than Flaubert says. He is content with "aux fulgurations de l'heure présente," he doesn't load the dice with an adjective to double-dazzle the noun. The "fulgurations" are allowed to shine, but their brilliance is not made crass or self-defeating. The eloquence of the whole passage is impartial, in keeping with Flaubert's determination to "write the mediocre well."[18] Every detail is culturally significant, but Flaubert doesn't nudge the reader.

It may be said that the scene is just another instance of Flaubert's realism: he is merely adding further items to what we already know, and trusting to the power of resemblance to do all the work. He has much the same sense of "the real" as Henry

James had when he distinguished between the real and the romantic:

> The real represents to my perception the things we cannot possibly *not* know, sooner or later, in one way or another; it being but one of the accidents of our hampered state, and one of the incidents of their quantity and number, that particular instances have not yet come our way. The romantic stands, on the other hand, for the things that, with all the facilities in the world, all the wealth and all the courage and all the wit and all the adventure, we never *can* directly know; the things that can reach us only through the beautiful circuit and subterfuge of our thought and our desire.[19]

But even if we cannot possibly *not* know that it was the custom of the country ("Selon la mode de la campagne") on a French farm to offer a visiting doctor something to drink, that knowledge doesn't get us far toward the liqueur glasses, one full, the other nearly empty, Emma's lips, her taut neck, her laughter, her beautiful teeth, her tongue licking the bottom of the glass, her cheeks, the palms of her hands, her cooling them on the knobs of the firedogs. Realism—which Flaubert professed to hate—is a genre of presentation, but it does not ordain what will be presented or how, what relations one constituent will bear to the others. Flaubert, not Emma, is in charge, and he gives every appearance of impartiality. It is as if he were willing to have these lives present themselves, employing him as a scribe, taking dictation. *Le mot juste* is the happy companion of good penmanship. But in turn, this was his way of getting rid of his responsibilities to his subject matter, by maintaining his aesthetic pride, his *superbia*, in its presence. His songs without words are written by refusing to distinguish between high notes and low notes, *fortissimo* and *pianissimo,* by eschewing climaxes and diminuendos. He preserves his decorum, at least in *Madame Bovary,* as if his style were at every point the supreme—because resolutely neutral—form of his eloquence.

V

The characteristic quality of a song without words is that the text—poem, story, novel—seems to issue from something memorably done, and to make the words ancillary to that. In *The Castle* Kafka has Mizzi playing with Klamm's letter, during a long conversation between K. and the Superintendent, and folding it into the shape of a little boat—"aus dem sie ein Schiffchen geformt hatte." The words don't matter, they could easily have been replaced by different ones: what matters is the gesture, the little unpredictable thing done. The chain seems to be as strong as its strongest link and to sweep aside other considerations. In E. A. Robinson's poem "The Mill," everything issues from the one thing the miller says, "There are no millers any more." The statement is not especially eloquent in itself, but it is not "in itself," it brings to a conclusion everything telling in its context. There is no saying where those words have begun, but we know where they end. The fact that the poem begins with the miller's suicide and ends with his wife's fulfills the logic of his saying "There are no millers any more," even though another man who said the same thing might have evaded the logic of it by looking for another job. Here is the first stanza:

> The miller's wife had waited long,
>   The tea was cold, the fire was dead;
> And there might yet be nothing wrong
>   In how he went and what he said:
> "There are no millers any more,"

Was all that she had heard him say;
And he had lingered at the door
So long that it seemed yesterday.

"There are no millers any more" is only a little more pronounced than the rest of the poem; mainly because these are the only words spoken, and the lines surrounding have the drab force of inevitability about them. They seem to say only "It was so," a report that hardly needs to be emphasized by the iambic plod of the lines and the monosyllabic rhymes (except for the last word, *yesterday*). The hope held out by "And there might yet be nothing wrong / In how he went" is faint, just a slight lift of possibility above the flat certitudes. The poem is rich in things not said, not said even by the wife to herself when she finds her husband's body hanging from a beam in the mill. In the last of the three stanzas, what the wife feels stops short of speech, but it is decisive enough in subjunctive intent. The difference between the two suicides is that the wife's—though *would* is enough for the poem—leaves no trace. The stanza begins with a notion of the husband's corpse:

And if she thought it followed her,
She may have reasoned in the dark
That one way of the few there were
Would hide her and would leave no mark:
Black water, smooth above the weir
Like starry velvet in the night,
Though ruffled once, would soon appear
The same as ever to the sight.[20]

In "Like starry velvet in the night," the narrative voice is identifying itself with the wife's unspoken words—this is unlikely to have been her simile—and speaking on her behalf. Her life has hardly included much silk, smooth or ruffled. But it doesn't matter. The eloquence of the poem is in the life before and after speech, the fate of it, the domestic situation and the one thing said to issue from it.

VI

I have been referring to one kind of eloquence—eloquence of situation—and implying that it reaches us as an action, a gesture, like a painting that makes no claim for itself, no comment to explain its force: it is what we take it to be. The other extreme form of eloquence—I have called it, with Eliot, "incantation"—works from a different principle, that words alone are certain good, even if not good enough for all seasons. The two ways are different, at least in their extreme versions. They may be in conflict, as Geoffrey Hill presents them in the passage I've quoted from *The Lords of Limit*. But it is possible to find them at work together—though not simultaneously—in the same poem or story. One of Emily Dickinson's most compelling poems is a case in point:

> I heard a Fly buzz—when I died—
> The Stillness in the Room
> Was like the Stillness in the Air—
> Between the Heaves of Storm—
>
> The Eyes around—had wrung them dry—
> And Breaths were gathering firm
> For that last Onset—when the King
> Be witnessed—in the Room—
>
> I willed my Keepsakes—Signed away
> What portion of me be
> Assignable—and then it was
> There interposed a Fly—

With Blue—uncertain—stumbling Buzz—
Between the light—and me—
And then the Windows failed—and then
I could not see to see—[21]

All you have to do, being a genius, is to imagine what it would
be like to have died; then to recall—what else would be possible?—something that happened in your last hours—say, a fly
alighting on your pillow. You need the image, to begin with.
Words are hardly necessary, in principle, though they will be
all that is there in practice. Then you dissociate the death-
watchers into their parts—eyes, breaths—and reify death as
King. Making your will is almost an interlude, social and domestic, except for the nicety with which it is done—"What
portion of me be / Assignable." These comments are misleading.
Dickinson adjudicates the events, she doesn't merely mention
them. She mentions the fly in the first line, so it must be important, perhaps the most irrefutable sensory event in the whole
experience. "Interpose" gives the scale of the eruption. The fly
displaces the King, as Helen Vendler has pointed out.[22] We are
gathered together as the death watch, awaiting the King, and
what we get instead is a fly buzzing around the room. After the
first line, the fly seems to go away for nearly three stanzas—at
least we don't hear it—but then it returns as another instance of
"betweenness"—"between the light and me." Dickinson gives
it her own qualities of consciousness—"uncertain" and "stumbling." When life begins to lapse, she distances its failure, at-
tributing it to "the Windows." They fail. "And then I could not
see to see." This last line is an instance of eloquence entirely
verbal. It is impossible to say precisely what it means, the cog-
nitive or optical experience denoted, apart from the language
that enforces it. It would be difficult to say how "I could not see
to see" differs from "I could not see." Vendler takes the former

clause to signify "the speaker's closing fall into unconsciousness," and that is right, it is a normative way of putting the event. It is what we would say, were we giving an account of it. But it doesn't quite register what Dickinson has done by presenting the lapse from consciousness to unconsciousness—two states, after all—in the form of the same verb *to see*. A first kind of seeing should enable the second, as the move from the indicative mood to the infinitive entails. But if we "translate" these grammatical moods into corresponding states of mind, we separate them more firmly than the line does—"I could not see to see." Dickinson's gesture is entirely within language: its eloquence is just as much "at one" with the English language as alliteration, rhyme, assonance, or enjambment. I'm not sure that it raises questions of eloquence in exactly the same respects as incantation and the auditory imagination.

VII

The most eloquent song without words known to me is the silence with which Dido answers Aeneas's excuses in book VI of the *Aeneid*. In book IV she and Aeneas have become lovers, in an episode carefully arranged by Venus. Dido is passionately in love with Aeneas, but his love is such that it can take second place to his duty. He is instructed by Jupiter, through Mercury, to leave Carthage and build Rome. When Dido learns of his deception—"quis fallere possit amantem?" (IV.296)—she denounces him: "perfide" (IV.366).[23] He claims that he has not thought of their lovemaking as constituting marriage, and that he must fulfill his civil duty. Dido curses him and promises to pursue him as a shade. In the end she says: Go, then, chase Italy with the winds, seek kingdoms through the seas: "I, sequere Italiam ventis, pete regna per undas" (IV.381). But she falters, and enlists her sister Anna to persuade Aeneas to remain with her, at least for a while. But he has determined to leave. Dido then tells Anna a story to conceal her intention of killing herself. Seeing that Aeneas has put to sea, Dido throws herself on her sword.

In book VI Dido is in Hell. Aeneas addresses her, insisting that he had not intended to leave her but that the gods' orders could not be disobeyed. Besides, he did not think she would take his leaving so hard. Dido turns away without saying a word. He calls to her: Who are you running from? This is the last time Fate will let me speak to you—"Quem fugis? Extremum fato quod te alloquor hoc est." But it is hopeless. She turns away, fixes her eyes on the ground: her expression never changes, as if her eyes were made of flint or Marpesian marble. Without any emotion she walks away to the shadowy grove where her former husband Sychaeus will comfort her and respond to her love. Aeneas, struck by the injustice of fate, watches her with tears and pity:

> Ciebat
> Illa solo fixos oculos aversa tenebat,
> nec magis incepto vultum sermone mouetur,
> quam si dura silex aut stet Marpesia cautes.
> Tandem corripuit sese atque inimica refugit
> in nemus vmbriferum, coniunx vbi pristinus illi
> respondet curis aequatque Sychaeus amorem.
> Nec minus Aeneas, casu concussus iniquo,
> prosequitur lacrimis longe et miseratur euntem . . .
> *(VI.469–76)*

Dryden's translation reads:

> Disdainfully she look'd; then turning round,
> But fix'd her eyes unmov'd upon the ground,
> And what he says and swears, regards no more

Than the deaf rocks, when the loud billows roar;
But whirl'd away, to shun his hateful sight,
Hid in the forest and the shades of night;
Then sought Sichaeus thro' the shady grove,
Who answer'd all her cares, and equal'd all her love.[24]

In "What Is a Classic?" T. S. Eliot referred to this episode and interpreted Aeneas's part in it with notable charity:

> I have always thought the meeting of Aeneas with the shade of Dido, in book VI, not only one of the most poignant, but one of the most civilized passages in poetry. It is complex in meaning and economical in expression, for it not only tells us about the attitude of Dido—still more important is what it tells us about the attitude of Aeneas. Dido's behaviour appears almost as a projection of Aeneas's own conscience: this, we feel, is the way in which Aeneas's conscience would *expect* Dido to behave to him. The point, it seems to me, is not that Dido is unforgiving—though it is important that, instead of railing at him, she merely snubs him—perhaps the most telling snub in all poetry: what matters most is, that Aeneas does not forgive himself—and this, significantly, in spite of the fact of which he is well aware, that all that he has done has been in compliance with destiny, or in consequence of the machinations of gods who are themselves, we feel, only instruments of a greater inscrutable power.[25]

Dido railed at Aeneas in book IV. It is a crucial factor in the eloquence of the passage in book VI that she replaces railing by silence, a magnificent withholding of the expression of her powers. It is her turning away, her refusal to speak or even to listen to Aeneas further, that is eloquent. She does not stay for his belated answer. Another factor, equally to the point, is Virgil's handing over her reaction, her snub, to third-person narration; it mimes her keeping-her-distance in the refusal of speech. The propriety of her behavior—which I think is what Eliot admired in referring to the "civilized" quality of the episode—is marked by its being admitted to the community of third-person narrative. Dido has learned how to conduct herself, declining the luxury of vehemence. It is a property of songs-without-words that they make one think that in the beginning was the deed, not the word. The word does not even follow as the deed's phonetic shadow: it is as if it elected not to follow at all.

4

Like Something Almost Being Said

> The trees are coming into leaf
> Like something almost being said.
> —Philip Larkin, "The Trees"

I am attracted to ellipsis, to the unsaid, to suggestion, to eloquent, deliberate silence. The unsaid, for me, exerts great power: often I wish an entire poem could be made in this vocabulary. It is analogous to the unseen; for example, to the power of ruins, to works of art either damaged or incomplete. Such works inevitably allude to larger contexts; they haunt because they are not whole, though wholeness is implied: another time, a world in which they were whole, or were to have been whole, is implied. There is no moment in which their first home is felt to be the museum.
—Louise Glück, "Disruption, Hesitation, Silence"

I

This chapter is likely to be irritating, because I try in it to say something more about a kind of eloquence that seems to issue from under the words and nearly apart from them and yet in the event is helplessly verbal. I take up where the previous chapter left off, but with no hope of making a consecutive argument. I'm just trying again. I choose several occasions or provocations, starting with one—Augustine's *De Musica*—that is nearly beyond or beneath comprehension, because it presents a kind of thinking that is gone, or so nearly gone from current speech that it requires special effort even to indicate where it was last seen. I quote R. P. Blackmur at length because he, more than any other modern critic, had a sense of the sublime not as something that may be reached by stretching out one's hand but as something that requires, even to gain a glimpse of it, many acts of divination or the experimental imagination.

Thinking of eloquence, Blackmur referred to "those deep skills of imagination by which we get into words what, when it is there, makes them memorable, and what, when it is gone, makes them empty."[1] The context of that observation was his reading of a strange little book, *St. Augustine's De Musica: A Synopsis* by W. F. Jackson Knight, published in London in 1949 by the Orthological Institute, then directed by C. K. Ogden. Knight wrote a synopsis rather than a full edition and translation of Augustine's treatise because of the constraints on scholarly work during the war. The synopsis gives more than the gist of Augustine's thought but less than a complete and exact rendering: near the end, it becomes virtually a paraphrase. (A scholarly edition of the sixth and last book of *De Musica*, the most inspiring part of it, has now been published.[2])

The treatise begins with a conspectus of the meters of Latin poetry and proceeds to distinguish the several kinds of rhythm, their particular impulses and capacities. There are three kinds, apparently, "rhythm in memory, rhythm in perception, and rhythm in sound." Rhythm "existing in silence is freer than rhythm created or extended not only in response to, *ad,* the body, but even in response to, *adversus,* the affects, *passiones,* of the body." For a while in the treatise, it appears that there are five kinds of rhythm, each of them a different manifestation of one nature, the soul or psyche. Augustine names them, but I don't need to, because he changes his mind on two of them and eventually finds a sixth kind, mainly by thinking that behind the five there must be a further, ultimate one to guarantee them. He then judges the several rhythms in relation to the soul's desire for order and finally for the presence of God. The treatise ends with a claim that earth, water, air, and sky—in ascending degrees of excellence—exhibit unity. This is Knight's version in the synopsis:

> Anything which the ministry of carnal perception can count, and anything contained in it, cannot be furnished with, or possess, any numerical rhythm in space which can be estimated, unless previously a numerical rhythm in time has preceded in silent movement. Before even that, there comes vital movement, agile with temporal intervals, and it modifies what it finds, serving the Lord of All Things. Its numerical structure is undistributed into intervals of time; the durations are supplied by potentiality; here, beyond, *supra quam,* even the rational and intellectual rhythm of blessed and saintly souls, here is the very Law of God, by which a leaf falls not, and for which, *cui,* the very hairs of our head are numbered; and, no nature intervening, *excipientes,* they transmit them to the law of earth, and the law below.[3]

The phrase that inspired Blackmur and stayed in his mind for several contexts was "agile with temporal intervals." A literal translation is not as thrilling. The Latin reads:

> Ista certe omnia, quae carnalis sensus ministerio numeramus, et quaecumque in eis sunt, locales numeros, qui uidentur esse in aliquo statu, nisi praecedentibus intimis in silentio temporalibus numeris, qui sunt in motu, nec accipere possunt nec habere. Illos itidem in temporum interuallis agiles praecedit et modificat uitalis motus seruiens Domino rerum

omnium, non temporalia habens digesta interualla numerorum suorum sed tempora ministrante
potentia, supra quam rationales et intellectuales nu-
meri beatarum animarum atque sanctarum legem
ipsam Dei, sine qua folium de arbore non cadit, et
cui nostri capilli numerati sunt, nulla interposita
natura excipientes usque ad terrena et inferna iura
transmittunt.[4]

Literally translated:

Surely, all these things, which we enumerate with
the aid of the carnal sense, and all things in them,
can neither receive nor possess any local rhythms,
which seem to be motionless, unless the innermost
temporal rhythms, which are in motion, silently
precede. These, which are mobile likewise in the
temporal intervals, are preceded and modified by a
vital movement which serves the Lord of all things,
without having distributed the temporal intervals
of its rhythms, but with a power that gives the
times, over which power the rational and intellectual rhythms of the blessed and holy souls without
any intervening nature receive the law of God—
without which not a single leaf falls from a tree and
for whom our hairs are counted—and transmit it to
the earthly and infernal laws.[5]

"Agile with temporal intervals" is a suggestive phrase, whatever
it means. If the Latin were strictly translated, the phrase should
not qualify the "vital movement" but the "innermost temporal rhythms." These, as the literal translation has it, are "mobile
likewise in the temporal intervals," whatever that, too, means.
Other phrases in the synopsis might have caught Blackmur's

attention, but didn't: "the durations are supplied by potentiality" is exotic, but hardly a close translation of "non temporalia habens digesta interualla numerorum suorum sed tempora ministrante potentia." The literal "without having distributed the temporal intervals of its rhythms, but with a power that gives the times" is not much clearer, even if we keep in mind that *tempora* is taken to mean times in the sense of temporal units or durations.

Blackmur does not claim to know what "agile with temporal intervals" means. The phrase has an air of significance, rather than a local meaning that could be attested. He uses it as a mantra, reciting it on the conviction that the recitation will yield eloquence beyond the mere call of duty. He doesn't seem troubled by its opacity. He has Augustine's authority—or thinks he has—to assume that "the patterns of number, in poetry and music, serve as reminders of the skills of thought which have nothing to do with the language of words." Augustine thinks that the meanings of words are arbitrary, "and by human authority," while the meanings of things, such as those which numbers move, are true, given by God. Blackmur comments:

> The music or the meaning, to paraphrase Eliot, is what goes on after the words have stopped; to Augustine the numbers made the form of the meaning according to laws which, with licenses of silence and elision allowed for, were absolute, were of interest in verse because of universal application, and were themselves a kind of limit to human knowledge. This is his way of claiming poetry as a form of knowledge, a form of being, or a form of revelation; claims to which we are sufficiently used in our own time.[6]

Presumably "what goes on after the words have stopped" is their echo or reverberation, in the sense in which a visual image may have an afterimage, retained by one's memory. Blackmur returned to "agile with temporal intervals" a few years later in "The Language of Silence" and said that Augustine knows "that thought does not take place in words—though it is administered and partly communicated in words, and is by fiction often present in them, and though, so to speak, it creates them, and creates further what they do to each other":

> Surely no one ever seriously thought words were autonomous. The story of the tower of Babel should have broken that fiction: every man speaks the language he can, and the angels understand them all. . . . Half the labor of writing is to exclude the wrong meanings from our words; the other half is to draw on the riches which have already been put into the words of our choice; and neither labor is effective unless the third thing is done—unless we put into the arrangement, the ordinance of our words, our own vital movement—"agile with temporal intervals."

It appears that "our own vital movement" is what Blackmur elsewhere calls gesture, one's force beneath and prior to the words with which we try to express it. That is its relation to silence, which is not the mere absence of speech but the action of the rhythm which is freer, as Augustine says, while it exists in silence than rhythm created or extended in response to the body or the affects of the body. Hence, as Blackmur says, "the positive obscurity of the greatest poetry in the words and hence the terrible clarity under them, pushing through."[7] The clarity under the words is terrible, I assume, because it exists only as unmoored force and not—or not yet—as speech. It is not terrible when we sense it in music, landscape painting, sculpture, and dance, because in these arts the cries are not expected to reach us in words. In music, silence has its place as the rest, which is just as significant—Morton Feldman's music being only an extreme instance of this—as the notes that come before and after it, just as much involved with memory and apprehension.[8]

"Vital movement, agile with temporal intervals," silence, and gesture: Blackmur resorts to occasions of these to achieve his own eloquence by exceeding them, driving them beyond their official selves. All the better when the occasions are incomplete, archaic torsos, suggestive rather than definitive, leaving him all the space in the world to give them his own form of completion or transcendence. I'll look at two or three of these in which what is given in the words is not quite said and we are left, without an enhanced reason, to our own devices.

II

In book II, chapter 20 of *Middlemarch,* Dorothea Casaubon, five weeks into her honeymoon in Rome, tries to divert her unhappiness by driving out to the Campagna. (The scene, much indebted to a corresponding one in *Little Dorrit,* impelled Henry James, in turn, to ascribe another version of it to Isabel Archer in *The Portrait of a Lady.*) There she sees, with confusion and dismay, the ruins of ancient Rome "set in the midst of a sordid present, where all that was living and warm-blooded seemed sunk in the deep degeneracy of a superstition divorced from reverence." *Seemed* is implausible. George Eliot is doing Dorothea's feeling for her and giving her words that she would not have found in her own stored intelligence. Eliot is ascribing her own antipathies to the poor girl. In the next paragraph she offers some general reflections:

> Not that this inward amazement of Dorothea's was anything very exceptional: many souls in their young nudity are tumbled out among incongruities and left to "find their feet" among them, while their elders go about their business. Nor can I suppose that when Mrs Casaubon is discovered in a fit of weeping six weeks after her wedding, the situation will be regarded as tragic. Some discouragement, some faintness of heart at the new real future which replaces the imaginary, is not unusual, and we do not expect people to be deeply moved by what is not unusual. That element of tragedy which lies in the very fact of frequency, has not yet wrought itself into the coarse emotion of mankind; and perhaps our frames could hardly bear much of it. If we had a keen vision and feeling of all ordinary human life, it would be like hearing the grass grow and the squirrel's heart beat, and we should die of that roar which lies on the other side of silence. As it is, the quickest of us walk about well wadded with stupidity.

In the next paragraph, Eliot writes of Dorothea:

> Permanent rebellion, the disorder of a life without some loving reverent resolve, was not possible to her; but she was now in an interval when the very force of her nature heightened its confusion.[9]

It is incompatible with the rhetoric of the first paragraph that we should ask what precisely is that roar, and where is the silence, and where is the other side of it, and how could a roar lie there, and what is the relation between the roar and the silence. In *The Marriage of Heaven and Hell* Blake says that if the doors of perception were cleansed, everything would appear to man as it is, infinite. This is much the same idea as Eliot's, but it leads to the opposite conclusion: one is not required to die of infinitude. We are supposed to read Eliot's sentence as issuing from the novelist's sense of horror at the frequency of marital woe and her equivocal feeling that we are fortunate in not having much of that sense; it is equivocal, because we have to be grateful for being stupid, and yet our stupidity is deplorable. If I have to interpret the sentence rather than take it as dear, gorgeous nonsense, I might say that the roar is the sum of human misery, *fortissimo*, which my intensified sense of hearing would apprehend, and silence is the domestic economy I practice to avoid the horror of such experience. But that is only one interpretation.

Blackmur puts the two paragraphs together and asks: "What was this force but that roaring?" And he goes on, rising to his own eloquence by striving to be equal to Eliot's and Tolstoi's:

> What was this force but that roaring? Tolstoi would have made the identification absolute; and it is a pity we do not have the language of his silence available. But Ivan Ilyitch heard the force roaring; and Dorothea is an Anna Karenina, only saved by the machinations of English novelistic conventions. The reader meditating the possibility does not require salvation; he requires a further flight of reason; for it is exactly here that George Eliot refuses a further screening and obscuring of reason. "Permanent rebellion" without resolve is one of the regular conditions of life. Reason must find it, for only rea-

son can deal with it, and reason is not reason unless it does so: it is mere dead reason, the course of inert ideas and anaesthetized sentiments, the rubbish of lost knowledge. But she is nevertheless presenting the experience of reason, not only here but again and again.[10]

The "screening and obscuring of reason" comes from another of Blackmur's experimental citations, two or three paragraphs back, Lu Chi's *Wen Fu:* "Reason screened and obscured begins to creep forth, thought comes screaming, forced out from the womb."[11]

George Eliot's "roar" seems to be something external and incorrigible, one of the tragic conditions of life, which we could sense only with renewed eyes and ears alert beyond accounting. Blackmur identifies the roar with "the very force of [Dorothea's] nature." This is convincing only if we take that force to be Dorothea's fate—which it may be; or if we take it as Dorothea's "vital movement, agile with temporal intervals," which she is driven to exert rather than a rough force necessarily exerted on her from without. The difference between the two interpretations is that Blackmur is not troubled by the ambiguity of Eliot's meaning—as the first interpretation is—because his impelling interest is to press so hard on her phrases that the consequence of his pressure will be his own expression, not utterly independent of hers but, in its smaller way, a new instance of eloquence. It is as if the Muse gave inspiration to her devotees not in a single great rush but in phrases, here and there, for those servants on the lookout for them. Blackmur needed instances of "something almost being said" as incitements, holding out the possibility that his eloquence will say something more or other.

III

In an essay, "On Not Knowing Greek," Virginia Woolf presents the Greek language, and especially that of Greek tragedy, as a kind of Ur-language—corresponding to Hebrew, I think, in another tradition—the speech of an unpolluted world and an unbroken humankind, a world ineffably different from our own. We are—she doesn't quite say this—mere Romans, worldly, bureaucratic, we coincide with our world and may be equal to it, but Greek testifies to a mode of life beyond the given discourses and the known qualities of eloquence:[12]

> If then in Sophocles the play is concentrated in the figures themselves, and in Euripides is to be retrieved from flashes of poetry and questions far flung and unanswered, Aeschylus makes these little dramas (the *Agamemnon* has 1663 lines; *Lear* about 2600), tremendous by stretching every phrase to the utmost, by sending them floating forth in metaphors, by bidding them rise and stalk eyeless and majestic through the scene. To understand him it is not so necessary to understand Greek as to understand poetry. It is necessary to take that dangerous leap through the air without the support of words which Shakespeare also asks of us. For words, when opposed to such a blast of meaning, must give out, must be blown astray, and only by collecting in companies convey the meaning which each one separately is too weak to express. Connecting them in a rapid flight of the mind we know instantly and instinctively what they mean, but could not decant that meaning afresh into any other words. There is an ambiguity which is the mark of the highest

poetry; we cannot know exactly what it means. Take this from the *Agamemnon* for instance—

ὀμμάτων δ' ἐν ἀχηνίαις ἔρρει πᾶσ' Ἀφροδίτα.

The meaning is just on the far side of language. It is the meaning which in moments of astonishing excitement and stress we perceive in our minds without words; it is the meaning that Dostoevsky (hampered as he was by prose and as we are by translation) leads us to by some astonishing run up the scale of emotions and points at but cannot indicate; the meaning that Shakespeare succeeds in snaring.[13]

Snaring doesn't seem the right word: that isn't what Shakespeare does. "The meaning is just on the far side of language" is as opaque as the passage I've quoted from *Middlemarch*. It presupposes in Woolf a secular form of mysticism in which a spatial sense of language assumes that there is an outer place beyond all words. In *The Waves* and other novels, she often has her characters brood over the limitations of language and meditate on whatever mode of being transcends everything that may be expressed. But even if Shakespeare alone can capture "the meaning," it is not beyond language. It is not clear how the line from the *Agamemnon*—or rather the lines, because Woolf runs lines 427 and 428 together—justify her excursus. In Eduard Fraenkel's translation, the Chorus bewails the fate of Menelaus after Helen's departure and before he leaves for Troy:

> Alas, alas for the house, alas for the princes! Alas for the bed and the husband-loving steps! One may see the silence of those who are forsaken, a silence without honour, without reviling, without belief. Through longing for her who is beyond the sea, a

phantom will seem to rule the house. The grace of
shapely statues is hateful to the husband, and when
the eyes are starved, all charm of love is gone.[14]

Woolf doesn't say what she takes Aeschylus to mean by "when
the eyes are starved, all charm of love is gone." More literally:
"and all Aphrodite/sexual attraction disappears in the *axhēniais*
of eyes." There are several possible nuances. The statues in the
house are hateful to Menelaus, in the absence of the real Helen.
Or: the phantom that seems to rule the house, now that Helen
is gone, is hateful to him. Or: Menelaus's eyes, deprived of
Helen, are immune to the beauty of the statues. Or: the statues
of Helen in the house torment Menelaus. This last is the translation arrived at by Alan Shapiro and Peter Burian:

> Alas,
> alas for the great house, for the house
> and for the princes! Alas for the lawful
> love-bed she once slipped eagerly into.
> See how he sits alone in such
> dishonored silence that he neither
> implores nor curses; and how, as he longs
> for her so far beyond the sea,
> a ghost is mistress of his house.
>> The chiselled flow of all
>> her flowing forms torments him;
>> against the void her eyes
>> leave, love is powerless.[15]

Woolf doesn't say how she construes Aeschylus's lines. "The
meaning is just on the far side of language" may indicate that to
her the emotional situation in Menelaus's house is so extreme
that her sense of it exceeds the words given to denote it. In the
years before and after the publication of Empson's *Seven Types*

of Ambiguity (1930) it was common to emphasize the ambiguity of literature and to rise to one's own little eloquence by acknowledging it. Here, Virginia Woolf seems to intuit the scene in Menelaus's house as if she saw it out of the corner of her eye and almost as if she had finished with the mere words. I don't understand how she could "take that dangerous leap through the air without the support of words" or how Blackmur can be so sure that thought can go on without words. But in any case Woolf achieves the eloquence of her commentary on the passage by almost—almost, but not quite—writing independently of the words that provoked it.

IV

Henry James's story "The Next Time" tells of a novelist, Ray Limbert, who tries, every year or so, to write a popular novel for the support of his wife and family but is prevented from achieving his end by the exacting quality of his imagination. In an age of "trash triumphant"—we might think of Gissing's *New Grub Street*—he can't bring himself to write fiction that the reading public will buy, though he is determined to make every effort. "I must cultivate the market—it's a science like another." "I haven't been obvious—I must *be* obvious. I haven't been popular—I must *be* popular." Limbert's sister is a popular novelist who couldn't fail with the public even if she tried. The narrator is also a writer, and while he wants Limbert to be a success, he doesn't want him to be low. He need not have worried. The novel that Limbert had designed for the market turned out otherwise. The narrator reports of it: "The thing was charming with all his charm and powerful with all his power: it was an unscrupulous, an unsparing, a shameless, merciless masterpiece." Of course the book is a failure, it doesn't sell, Limbert has keyed it up too high. But he will persist. The narrator says:

He'll try again for the common with what he'll believe to be a still more infernal cunning, and again
the common will fatally elude him, for his infernal
cunning will have been only his genius in an inef-
fectual disguise.

It is impossible to understand "why the note [Limbert] strained
every chord to pitch for common ears should invariably insist
on addressing itself to the angels." His wife decides that "one
really had to think him a very great man because if one didn't
one would be rather ashamed of him." He tries again with a
novel called *The Hidden Heart*, to the same grim result. Meanwhile, he has contracted rheumatic fever, so he must exert himself for a last appeal to the market. He starts upon a novel called
Derogation, but this time he consults mainly his own talent and
its inclination. The narrator visits him:

> I got a strange, stirring sense that he had not con-
> sulted the usual [omens] and indeed that he had
> floated away into a grand indifference, into a reck-
> less consciousness of art. The voice of the market
> had suddenly grown faint and far: he had come
> back at the last, as people so often do, to one of the
> moods, the sincerities of his prime. Was he really
> with a blurred sense of the urgent doing something
> now only for himself? We wondered and waited—
> we felt that he was a little confused. What had hap-
> pened, I was afterwards satisfied, was that he had
> quite forgotten whether he generally sold or not.
> He had merely waked up one morning again in
> the country of the blue and had stayed there with
> a good conscience and a great idea. He stayed till
> death knocked at the gate, for the pen dropped

from his hand only at the moment when from sudden failure of the heart his eyes, as he sank back in
his chair, closed for ever. *Derogation* is a splendid
fragment; it evidently would have been one of his
high successes. I am not prepared to say it would
have waked up the libraries.[16]

The narrator means the lending libraries.

Blackmur does not press as hard for eloquence on "the country of the blue" as he does on George Eliot's "roar on the other
side of silence" and Augustine's "agile with temporal intervals." He doesn't need to. Up to a point, the meaning is clear.
In the case of an artist of Ray Limbert's quality, there is always
something that can be called his country, whether it is "of the
blue" or another color. Blackmur considers "The Next Time"
along with several other stories—"The Figure in the Carpet,"
"The Private Life," "The Death of the Lion," "The Great Good
Place," and "The Lesson of the Master"—as fables of the artis-
tic life, of artists who are doomed "either because they cannot
meet the conditions of life imposed upon them by society or
because society will have none of them no matter how hard they
try." The country of the blue is, he says, "a very lonely place to
be, for it is very nearly empty except for the self, and is gained
only by something like a religious retreat, by an approximation
of birth or death or birth-in-death":

> Yet there was some constant recourse for James
> to the country of the blue; it was where he would
> have had his projected great authors live, and it was
> where . . . he sometimes lived himself.

Blackmur does not mean Rye. If an artist is true and sees truly,
as he says, "his vision disappears in his work, which is the country of the blue."[17] Where else could it be? If we wanted further

assurance of this from James, we could turn to the preface to *The Tragic Muse*, where we find him saying:

> Any presentation of the artist *in triumph* must be flat in proportion as it really sticks to its subject—it can only smuggle in relief and variety. For, to put the matter in an image, all we then—in his triumph—see of the charm-compeller is the back he turns to us as he bends over his work.[18]

But that does not make the work or the workplace blue.

Presumably the country of the blue is the place in which the creative imagination finds itself not thwarted or humiliated but free. Sometimes it is given a specific and congenial name, as in Verlaine's "Qu'il était bleu, le ciel, et grand, l'espoir!"[19] More often, as in "The Next Time," we are allowed to fill the space with whatever moral or aesthetic qualities we think appropriate. William H. Gass thought the space so inspiringly open that he wrote *On Being Blue: A Philosophical Inquiry* to respond to its invitation. He starts with blue pencils and lists more instances of blue, many of them naughty, than you would have thought probable, including the version of blue in "The Next Time." Among the decent texts he quotes there is Stevens's "The Man with the Blue Guitar" but not T. S. Eliot's "In blue of larkspur, blue of Mary's colour." What Gass says of Limbert's "country of the blue" goes beyond my knowledge and therefore may be taken as true or not:

> Blue as you enter it disappears. Red never does that. Every article of air might look like cobalt if we got outside ourselves to see it. The country of the blue is clear.

Sky blue, maybe. Near the end of *On Being Blue* Gass resolves the question of blue—but in a way that gives us a new problem to replace the old one—by urging writers to "give up the blue things of this world in favor of the words which say them," whereupon we are back not with blue pencils but with the words "blue pencils" and so forth to other words. The book, he says, "was written for all those who live in the country of the blue," but that is not quite the end of the said-and-written sentence.[20] Gass appears to believe, with Yeats's Happy Shepherd, that "Words alone are certain good."[21]

V

In act 3, scene 1 we hear that the king has sent for Hamlet and arranged that he will meet Ophelia "as 'twere by accident." Polonius gives her a book of devotions to read, so that Hamlet will not wonder why she is alone. The king and Polonius then withdraw so that they can spy upon the encounter. Hamlet enters and speaks the "To be, or not to be" soliloquy. He has not yet seen Ophelia. When he does—

> Soft you now!
> The fair Ophelia! Nymph, in thy orisons
> Be all my sins rememb'red . . .

—to which she answers—

> Good my lord,
> How does your honour for this many a day?
> *(3.1.88–91)*

It is up to the actors to interpret this exchange and the several exchanges that ensue. Hamlet's "Nymph, in thy orisons" may be enough to refuse intimacy, a refusal to which Ophelia responds in kind with the distancing formality of "How does your honour for this many a day?" The encounter goes quickly by going badly. Ophelia insists on returning Hamlet's gifts, and he insults her with low talk of *honest* and *fair,* till he leaves her, shouting the madness of "To a nunnery, go." Ophelia then has a speech of twelve lines to fill the interval until the king and Polonius enter again:

> O, what a noble mind is here o'er-thrown!
> The courtier's, soldier's, scholar's, eye, tongue, sword;
> Th' expectancy and rose of the fair state,
> The glass of fashion and the mould of form,
> Th' observ'd of all observers, quite, quite, down!
> And I, of ladies most deject and wretched,
> That suck'd the honey of his music vows,
> Now see that noble and most sovereign reason,
> Like sweet bells jangled, out of time and harsh;
> That unmatch'd form and feature of blown youth
> Blasted with ecstasy: O, woe is me,
> T' have seen what I have seen, see what I see!
> *(3.1.158–69)*

A short speech, but it goes all the way from theatricality to absorption. I take these terms from Michael Fried's description of two conventions in French painting. Theatricality is the mode of painting in which the figures are lined up before us "so we might look at them . . . so they might be beheld." It assumes that a painting is meant to be looked at, as if it were a face to be acknowledged or confronted. Manet's *The Old Musician* and *Le Déjeuner sur l'herbe* are instances. Absorption is the mode of painting in which the figures are so absorbed in what they are doing that they are "unaware of the presence before the canvas of the beholder." They are examples of what Fried calls "the blindness to being beheld," as in Fantin-Latour's *Woman Reading* and Millet's *The Gleaners, The Angelus,* and *The Vineyard Worker.*[22] The first line of Ophelia's speech is directed to the audience: "O, what a noble mind is *here* o'er-thrown." The allusion to courtier, soldier, and scholar is a public one, civic in its range: the audience is expected to know what these roles entail. "Th' expectancy and rose of the fair state" is a feature of Shakespeare's style rather than of Ophelia's: he was fond of such doubling of nouns, especially when one of them was Latin, abstract, and polysyllabic and the other a simple monosyllable. Fond, too, of making his listeners think as well as see.[23] But the speech is not merely external or choric: "quite, quite, down!" issues from Ophelia, not from reportage. "And I, of ladies most deject and wretched"—another doubling, this time of adjectives—is also a theatrical expostulation, in strong contrast to Hamlet's soliloquy that is still in our ears, although Hamlet spoke of "we" and "us," not of "I." But Ophelia's speech ends in absorption so inward that she can hardly even be said to be talking to herself: "O, woe is me, / T' have seen what I have seen, see what I see." She is no longer addressing an audience: she is musing the obscurity of her woe. The four stressed forms of the verb *to see* and the division of the verse line into two coordinate parts indicate the locked-in nature of her consciousness. What she has seen is Hamlet, out of his mind. What she sees is indeterminate, it is beyond what she has seen, though we can't know how far. The eloquence of the lines is *pianissimo*, Ophelia is sinking into herself as if words could go no further and must end in defeated silence. Or as if language at the end of its tether said: "There is more, but it can't be said; not yet." Ophelia is absorbed in her perception, such that there is no one present to her but herself. When the king and Polonius enter, we have an abrupt change: "Love! his affections do not that way tend."

When Blackmur quotes "T' have seen what I have seen, see what I see!" as he often does, he takes the line as text for a parable about the mutual impingement, in literature, of behavior and morals. "Behaviour is the medium in which our lives take place." Literature and religion—which he sometimes speaks of instead of morals—give us "theoretic forms of our lives seen as behaviour." They give us, "between them, with ferocity of observation and charity of apprehension, almost the only secure knowledge we have of what happens to our mind and our spirit when we behave as the wind behaves." Hamlet's behavior in act 3, scene 1 is like the wind's behavior, swirling words, insults, tirades. Ophelia's speech brings morals and manners to bear upon him, gives theoretic form to his behavior: "She looks everywhere about her, for she contains in her own way everything she sees."[24] The only point I would add is that the theoretic form culminates in her internalizing of the behavior and of the morality and manners she exerts upon it. It is theoretic—Blackmur takes the notion of theoretic form from Croce's *Aesthetic*—because the values to which it appeals are public, and not immediately applicable to the behavior they address.

VI

Seamus Heaney's *The Haw Lantern* (1987) contains a sequence of poems called "Clearances," numbered 1 to 8 with an unnumbered one in italics to start it off. The sequence makes an elegy in memory of Heaney's mother, "M.K.H. 1911–1984." The last poem in the group refers to its predecessor and "the space we stood around" where the woman died in her bed, a space "emptied/Into us to keep."[25] The poet recalls the tree he grew from a chestnut and planted in a jam jar in the garden. The basis of the poem is a comparison between the chestnut tree, cut down after many years to make room for something else, and the woman's life, cut down for no clear reason except that every life must end. Common to both is the space they leave, which the poet is impelled to fill with his elegiac meditations. The space left by the dead woman is "utterly empty," and yet, because it can't be accepted in that penury, it must be imagined as a place of further possibility, a source. The woman, like the tree, is gone, but not absolutely gone: something must remain, corresponding to her son's desire to walk round and round the space. In an elegy, it is permissible to indulge the "pathetic fallacy," according to the poetic convention by which Nature, too, mourns, like the bereaved one. The "sigh" is a breath in common, the shock of the "shocked tips" is first the poet's, then an apparition transferred to the tree. The feeling is well measured, but not so definitively that it may be packed up and left to fend for itself. "Its heft and hush become a bright nowhere": noun and adjective in that last phrase pull against each other while staying, each of them, in place. The chestnut tree becomes the woman's soul and gains eternal life, according to a convention of elegy and an article of faith in Roman Catholicism.

But then there is the something almost being said—"A soul ramifying and forever / Silent, beyond silence listened for." Most of the work is done by *beyond*, creating a space and projecting a further, rarefied place beyond it. The silence we listen for is of our ordinary world, as when a car passes along a country road and we wait for the noise of it to cease. "Beyond silence listened for" is a further range, not of our ordinary world but of our aspiration, as a Catholic believes in a next world and distinguishes between body and soul, the latter—we hope and pray—its redeemed inhabitant. A not entirely secular precedent for this is given in Keats's "Ode on a Grecian Urn":

> Heard melodies are sweet, but those unheard
> Are sweeter; therefore, ye soft pipes, play on;
> Not to the sensual ear, but, more endeared,
> Pipe to the spirit ditties of no tone.[26]

The pipes come from the first stanza, "What pipes and timbrels?" The relation between the sensual ear and the spirit, as Kenneth Burke interpreted it, corresponds to that between sound as we hear it and absolute sound, the essence of sound "which would be soundless as the prime mover is motionless, or as the 'principle' of sweetness would not be sweet, having transcended sweetness."[27] We are dealing with motives-above-motives, passing from existence to essence, as the "heft and hush" of Heaney's chestnut tree are essentialized into "a bright nowhere," the essence of space, while he retains the sensory images of their one-time existence. The past participle—"Its heft and hush become a bright nowhere"—is extended into a continuous present participle—"ramifying" without limit—while the body is refined to soul, and every remembered sound of the mother becomes, like Keats's "ditties of no tone," silent in a silence-above-silence, beyond the worldly silence we merely listen for. The phrase "and forever / Silent" invokes the motive-above-the-given-motive without further specification.

No theory of communication is quite adequate to the last lines of the poem. I prefer a theory of invention, according to which the poet discovers possibilities within the verbal medium and seizes them, provided only that they do not suppress the other duties he has undertaken, notably those of an elegist. I am not claiming that the whole poem is discovered within the verbal medium: the world outside the poem, as well as inside it, contains mothers, gardens, chestnut trees, wallflowers, jam jars, and dyings that don't wait for words. A painter, having taken canvas, paints, and brushes into his hands, may discover possibilities of form and expression far beyond his intention. Something seems necessary or at least good—a gesture of paint and form—and the painter assents to it. In the last lines of Heaney's poem, something is almost being said, but not entirely. The something is at once in the words and a little beyond them. It is in the words as the slant rhyme of *fore*ver and listened *for*, both syllables rhyming—though differently—with the last syllable of *nowhere*, keeps the lines within language; and the keeping is

ensured by the progression from *silent* to *silence,* the noun held
in place by the motif word *beyond,* marking the enabling action
of the poem. But the something is not entirely specified, it is in
the shadow beyond the words, as we say that connotations are
slightly apart from the denotations that provoke them, or—as
in John Crowe Ransom's theory of literature—that texture is
permitted to be off to one side of the structure that has first
rights to the poem.

VII

Not everything that is said is said verbally: there are frowns,
significant smiles, cries and whispers, gestures that have cultural implications. What is said verbally is only a part of what,
in principle, might be said. At the end of *S/Z* Roland Barthes
takes up the last sentence of Balzac's *Sarrasine,* the story he
has been elucidating: "Et la marquise resta pensive." Perhaps
reflecting on one's common anxiety to have "the last word," he
thinks of an unspoken word beyond it:

> Like the Marquise, the classic text is pensive: re-
> plete with meaning (as we have seen), it still seems
> to be keeping in reserve some ultimate meaning [*un
> dernier sens*], one it does not express but the place
> of which it keeps free and signifying [*libre et sig-
> nifiante*]: this zero degree of meaning (which is not
> its annulment but on the contrary its recognition)
> [*la reconnaissance*], this supplementary, unexpected
> meaning which is the theatrical sign of the implicit,
> is pensiveness: the pensive (in faces, in texts) is the
> signifier of the inexpressible, not of the unexpressed.
> For if the classic text has nothing more to say than
> what it says, at least it attempts to "let it be under-

stood" that it does not say everything: this *allusion* is coded by pensiveness, which is a sign of nothing but itself: as though, having filled the text but obsessively fearing that it is not *incontestably* filled, the discourse insisted on supplementing it with an *et cetera* of plenitude. Just as the pensiveness of a face signals that this head is heavy with unspoken language, so the (classic) text inscribes within its system of signs the signature of its plenitude: like the face, the text becomes *expressive* (let us say that it signifies its expressivity), endowed with an interiority the supposed depth of which compensates for the parsimony of its plural [*de son pluriel*]. *What are you thinking of,* we want to ask the classic text, on its discreet urging; but the text, wilier than all those who try to escape by answering: *nothing,* does not reply, giving meaning its last closure: suspension.[28]

Barthes doesn't quite say where *un dernier sens* is located or even where it is to be sought. Suspension is for the moment his last word. But it might be called language, not language-as-such but the particular language in which the anterior words appear. This is Gadamer's way of addressing the issue:

But there is another dialectic of the word, which assigns to every word an inner dimension of multiplication: every word breaks forth as if from a centre and is related to a whole, through which alone it is a word. Every word causes the whole of the language to which it belongs to resonate and the whole of the view of the world which lies behind it to appear. Thus every word, in its momentariness, carries with it the unsaid, to which it is related by responding and indicating. The occasionality of human speech

is not a casual imperfection of its expressive power;
it is, rather, the logical expression of the living vir-
tuality of speech, that brings a totality of meaning
into play, without being able to express it totally.[29]

Pensiveness is Barthes's word, a gift from Balzac, for this sense
of expressive limitation: it indicates that one knows there is
more to be said though it can't be fully said. Barthes ascribes
this sense to a face, the face of a person in thought. Gadamer
ascribes it to the language spoken or written, a resource that
can't always be brought to the state of performance. Barthes's
sense of face consorts with self-containment, absorption: like
the figures in Yeats's "Long-Legged Fly"—Caesar, Helen of
Troy, Michelangelo—their minds moving upon silence, silence
as if it were a verb as well as a noun. Silence is what we often
call the not-quite-said, as Eliot in "Burnt Norton" writes:
"Words, after speech, reach / Into the silence."[30] As if to say
that words fail unless they find the providential form of themselves, the pattern, like that of a Chinese jar moving "perpetu-
ally in its stillness." The pattern does not cease to be material,
it is discovered in the material at hand. The Chinese jar is not
separate from the clay of which it is made: its form is a quality
of the clay, not a metaphysical datum beyond it. Eliot takes
care not to drive the consideration of form beyond reason or
into mysticism, as Wittgenstein does in a well-known passage
in the *Tractatus:*

> The inexpressible, indeed, exists [*Es gibt allerdings
> Unaussprechliches*]. It *shows itself*; it is the mystical.
> . . . Concerning that about which one cannot speak,
> one must remain silent.[31]

I don't understand how the status attributed here to "the in-
expressible" is that of existence. That it might be posited, and

held to be dependent on an act of positing, would seem to be enough.

VIII

Carol Shields's "Taking the Train" tells of Gweneth McGowan, an up and coming professor of English, visiting her friend Northie McCord in Calgary, Alberta. Northie's husband was mauled to death by a grizzly in a provincial park a year before. On this visit, Gweneth and Northie sit in the garden and talk of gone times while eating a meal prepared by Northie's fifteen-year-old daughter Gwen—cold sliced beef, potato salad, a fiery mustard, and iced tea. When the evening turns cold, Gwen goes into the house. Later, Gweneth and Northie follow her:

> When they came into the house, they found Gwen sitting on the living-room floor, listening to a Bruce Springsteen record, a long moaning song. She held up the record sleeve, which said: "New York City Serenade."
>
> "It's coming," she told the two of them as they stood in the doorway. "The best part is coming." She shut her eyes and held up a finger, just as the song changed abruptly from gravel-weighted melody to anguished wail and the repeated phrase, "She won't take the train, she won't take the train." Listening, her face went luminous with sorrow, and her lips mouthed the tragic words. "'No, she won't take the train, no, she won't take the train.'"
>
> Who won't take the train? Gweneth wanted to demand roughly. Why not? And did it matter? The mystery was that a phrase so rich with denial could enthrall a young girl.

We hear nothing further from Gwen or indeed from Springsteen; the last part of "New York City Serenade" escapes from the fixation of "Oh she won't take the train, no she won't take the train" and moves to another repeated line, "Listen to your junk man." The story ends with Gweneth still thinking about the girl:

> Gweneth felt an impulse to rescue her with logic, with exuberance, but stopped just in time. An image came into her mind, an old, traditional image of women who, after a meal, will take a tablecloth, shake it free of crumbs and put it away, each taking a corner, folding it once, then twice, then again. They never hesitate, these women, moving in and out, in and out, as skilled and graceful as dancers. And now, Gweneth thought: here we are, the three of us, holding on to this wailing rag-tag of music for all we're worth, and to something else that we can't put a name to, but don't dare drop.[32]

Why won't the woman take the train? In fact Springsteen gives the reason: "She's afraid them tracks are gonna slow her down." Gweneth doesn't hear the line, or if she does she doesn't understand it. Instead, her mind takes up the image of women folding a tablecloth. The only rational connection to this image is that women are holding something, a tablecloth, a rag-tag of music. "For all we're worth" marks the desperation of women bereft of traditions; they have nothing else to dance to. Gweneth holds the image in her mind, but there is also the space surrounding it, the "something else that we can't put a name to, but don't dare drop." The eloquence of Springsteen's song is in the little something understood and the force of all the things around it not understood. Shields's eloquence in the whole story is her sense—and Gweneth's—of all the nameless feelings surrounding the few we can put a name to. Why not drop them? That would make our lives even more weightless than they often seem to be.

IX

The chapter epigraph from Larkin's "The Trees" is, I hope, suggestive, but it is also misleading. The trees will soon come into leaf by force of nature, you have only to wait for them, but the something almost being said may never be said, it may have to stay in that "almost" condition, as if tonguetied. One of its social correlatives is the state of inarticulateness we often meet in life and nearly as often in Robert Frost's poems; as in "Out, Out—" when the boy whose hand has been severed by the buzz saw dies and, as Frost writes of the onlookers:

> And they, since they
> Were not the one dead, turned to their affairs.[33]

We don't know what any of these people might have said, but we are not justified in assuming that their failure to speak was a sign of their failure to feel. They may have felt just as acutely as the most articulate witness, though what they felt, we can't know. Frost is judiciously tender to such people, even when he also assents to those who have survived: there is a touch of the Social Darwinist in him. The reason he supplies in "Out, Out—" "since they/Were not the one dead" may strike us as cynical, but it is sadly convincing. "Turned" is what they must have done, could not otherwise have done. "To their affairs" is a distancing phrase, the plural a terrible acknowledgment of sundry.

Frost is eloquent in every mode of it, from the least means to the most; from "And to do that to birds was why she came" and "And what I would not part with I have kept" to "Provide, provide!" Eloquent himself, he is responsive to eloquence in others. When someone quoted to him the opening sentence of Emerson's Divinity School Address—"In this *refulgent* summer it has been a luxury to draw the breath of life"—and made much of the adjective, Frost remarked:

> Of course, anybody would sit up and take notice when a speaker began like that. Undoubtedly there's a freshness there in the use of that word that amounts to brilliance; but you ought not to use the word in just that way. Emerson made it his own; let it alone.[34]

That is sound advice, especially forceful coming as it does from the poet-critic who made an aesthetic of "sentence sounds." Frost is always ready to sit up and take notice. He is also remarkably alive to the pressure of those motives that try to force themselves up and out into the free air of expression, and often fail.

5

To Make an End

1

In this chapter I hope to draw attention to a particular form of eloquence that coincides with endings, moments in which a new direction is offered, if only as a relief from the old one, or a blessed release is provided in the feeling that the novel, poem, story, play, film is at last coming to an end.

The lawyer-narrator of "Bartleby, the Scrivener" receives a note from Bartleby's landlord: he has sent for the police and had the nuisance removed to the Tombs—the Halls of Justice—as a vagrant. The question of the legality of this proceeding is not raised. The same day, the lawyer goes to the Tombs to see Bartleby:

> Being under no disgraceful charge, and quite serene and harmless in all his ways, they had permitted him freely to wander about the prison, and especially in the inclosed grass-platted yards thereof. And so I found him there, standing all alone in the quietest of the yards, his face towards a high wall, while all around, from the narrow slits of the jail windows, I thought I saw peering out upon him the eyes of murderers and thieves.
>
> "Bartleby!"
>
> "I know you," he said, without looking round,— "and I want nothing to say to you."

We hear a new note in Bartleby's demeanor. Up to this point, his refusals—either to obey his employer or to yield to any request—have been consistent and unqualified, but civil. He has not been rancorous or even sullen. The note of complaint is a slight blemish in the telling of the story; it makes Bartleby appear for the first time commonplace, just as querulous as any of us would be in his circumstances. The lawyer protests, and commits the indelicacy of patronizing Bartleby:

> "It was not I that brought you here, Bartleby," said I, keenly pained at his implied suspicion. "And to you, this should not be so vile a place. Nothing reproachful attaches to you by being here. And see, it is not so sad a place as one might think. Look, there is the sky, and here is the grass."[1]

"To you" starts a line of vulgarity, extended in "And see" and "Look." Restoring himself to his proper tone, Bartleby answers: "I know where I am." The logic of the restoration is that he goes on hunger strike, silently, without threats or conditions.

Before leaving, the lawyer gives the grub-man some money to look after Bartleby and see that he is well fed. He returns a few days later:

> The yard was entirely quiet. It was not accessible to the common prisoners. The surrounding walls, of amazing thickness, kept off all sounds behind them. The Egyptian character of the masonry weighed upon me with its gloom. But a soft imprisoned turf grew under foot. The heart of the eternal pyramids, it seemed, wherein, by some strange magic, through the clefts, grass-seed, dropped by birds, had sprung.
>
> Strangely huddled at the base of the wall, his

knees drawn up, and lying on his side, his head touching the cold stones, I saw the wasted Bartleby. But nothing stirred. I paused; then went close up to him; stooped over, and saw that his dim eyes were open; otherwise he seemed profoundly sleeping. Something prompted me to touch him. I felt his hand, when a tingling shiver ran up my arm and down my spine to my feet.

The round face of the grub-man peered upon me now. "His dinner is ready. Won't he dine today, either? Or does he live without dining?"

"Lives without dining," said I, and closed the eyes.

"Eh!—He's asleep, aint he?"

"With kings and counselors," murmured I.[2]

After an ellipsis, the story ends with a long paragraph in which we are given the rumor that Bartleby had been employed as a subordinate clerk in the Dead Letter Office at Washington till a change in the administration cost him his job. "On errands of life, these letters speed to death." "Ah Bartleby! Ah humanity!" the story ends.

The implied acceptance with which we receive the story is intimated first by the "soft imprisoned turf" and the grass seed "dropped by birds," as if on creative purpose. But mostly it is elicited by the lawyer's response to the grub man's "He's asleep, aint he?": "With kings and counselors." Technically, it is a response to the grub man, but it is really the lawyer's murmur to himself: the grub man is unlikely to have read the Book of Job and caught the allusion to Job cursing his day:

Why died I not from the womb? *why* did I *not* give up the ghost when I came out of the belly?

Why did the knees prevent me? or why the
breasts that I should suck?
For now should I have lain still and been quiet, I
should have slept: then had I been at rest.
With kings and counsellors of the earth, which
built desolate places for themselves;
Or with princes that had gold, who filled their
houses with silver:
Or as an hidden untimely birth I had not been;
as infants *which* never saw light. (Job 3:11-16)

The eloquence of the lawyer's murmur consists in its removing
Bartleby's life-and-death from the state in which it merely coincides with itself and placing it—interring it—beside the lives
of Job and everyone else Job refers to: kings, counselors, princes,
and infants who never saw the light. Eloquence does not allow
anything to be merely itself; it enhances it, or condemns it, but
in any case changes it, bringing a larger perspective to bear. According to eloquence, nothing is what it merely or ostensibly is;
it is larger or smaller than that. In any event it is different, seen
differently. How far the eloquence goes, from its reference to
Job, is up to each reader. In the case of the grub man it probably
goes nowhere. There is no reason to think he understands what
the lawyer is saying. The rest of us make a little better showing.
The difference between Job and Bartleby is that Job complains
all the time; Bartleby doesn't. Like Job, Bartleby is both in the
right and the wrong. We sympathize with Job against God until
Job repents and God rewards him with riches and happiness.
We sympathize with Bartleby against the world, society, no-
body in particular. He must have his reason, though he doesn't
disclose it. William Empson said that Hamlet kept his secret
by telling everybody that he had one. Bartleby internalizes his
complaint; he doesn't show us his cause. We make of his life-

and-death whatever we can. The lawyer's eloquence at the end incites us to keep going, trying to make sense of it all. His allusion to Job's kings and counselors does not transcend Bartleby's death but sees it in a grand light. Like them, he has made a mess of his life; a mess is what we mostly make of it.

Jacques Derrida, comparing Bartleby to Job, says that the comparison is not "to him who hoped to join the kings and counsellors one day after his death, but to him who dreamed of not being born." That is plausible, though it prefers something the lawyer didn't quite say to what he said. But then Derrida goes on to suggest a comparison of Bartleby to Abraham:

> Just as Abraham doesn't speak a human language, just as he speaks in tongues, or in a language that is foreign to every other human language, and in order to do that responds without responding, speaks without saying anything either true or false, says nothing determinate that would be equivalent to a statement, a promise or a lie, in the same way Bartleby's "I would prefer not to" takes on the responsibility of a response without response. . . . We don't know what he wants or means to say, or what he doesn't want to do or say, but we are given to understand quite clearly that *he would prefer not to*.

In fact, we know exactly what Bartleby says: his statements are completed by the several requests made to him; in each case he prefers not to do what he has just then been asked to do. Derrida ends by interpreting a different story from the one that Melville wrote. Pursuing the comparison with Abraham:

> He [Abraham] would prefer that God didn't let him do it, that he would hold back his hand, that he would provide a lamb for the holocaust, that

the moment of this mad decision would lean on the side of nonsacrifice, once the sacrifice were to be accepted. He will not decide *not to,* he has decided *to,* but he would prefer not to. He can say nothing more and will do nothing more if God, if the Other, continues to lead him towards death, to the death that is offered as a gift. And Bartleby's "I would prefer not to" is also a sacrificial passion that will lead him to death, a death given by the law, by a society that doesn't even know why it acts the way it does.[3]

But there is nothing sacrificial about Bartleby's passion, no God exacts a sacrifice from him. Bartleby's death is not "given by the law," he is not executed for vagrancy, and society knows full well why it detains vagrants as it does (or once did: vagrancy is, so far as I know, no longer a crime unless it can be construed as "loitering with intent to commit a felony"). Bartleby goes on a starvation strike, not for a proclaimed cause—as in Northern Ireland Bobby Sands did—but presumably because he no longer wanted to live. Why he no longer wanted to live is open to any reader's speculation. If the mess I have made of my life is comprehensive, I may have no further interest in living.

The effect of the lawyer's "With kings and counselors" is to present Bartleby's life-and-death, like Job's, as a myth, a story told for the benefit of those to whom it is addressed. The story is to be received by the whole human community. That is the justification of the lawyer's last thought: "Ah Bartleby! Ah humanity!" His eloquence is the mythic reverberation he gives to a life-and-death that would otherwise be just another pathetic case.

The second part of *The Waste Land*—"A Game of Chess"—ends with a scene in an English public house. It is closing time, and the barman is urging the customers to leave. We hear bits of talk from an unnamed woman about Lil and her husband Albert, her bad teeth, her abortion, Albert's return from the war, the dinner of celebration. Then it's time to go:

> Goonight Bill. Goonight Lou. Goonight May.
> Goonight.
> Ta ta. Goonight. Goonight.

"A Game of Chess" could have ended there, like an episode of *Coronation Street* or *Eastenders*. Instead we have a final good-night in the last line: "Good night, ladies, good night, sweet ladies, good night, good night."[4] There is no logical call for it. In act 4, scene 5 of *Hamlet*, Ophelia enters to the queen and, a few moments later, the king: she is distracted, deranged by her father's death, and talks and sings a mixture of sense and non-sense, fragments of reason in madness. The little episode ends with her fantasy of herself as queen calling for her coach and saying farewell: "Come, my coach! Good night, ladies; good night, sweet ladies; good night, good night" (4.5.72–74). As in "Bartleby, the Scrivener," the eloquence of the allusion in *The Waste Land* removes the reader from the situation at hand, and brings a new and larger perspective to bear on it. The device is—in a phrase commonly ascribed to Marshall McLuhan— "juxtaposition without copula." It comes from abstract paint-ing, where a blob of paint on the canvas may be in some relation to another one, but the relation is not specified or even to be de-duced as in a realistic painting. No syntax links the constituents of abstraction: we make what we can of the painting without the guidance of its referring to anything in the common world.

In "A Game of Chess," one good-night leads to another on the poet's sole authority. Kenneth Burke has considered it in the "Psychology and Form" chapter of *Counter-Statement*, starting from the proposition that form is "the creation of an appetite in the mind of the auditor" or reader, "and the adequate satisfying of that appetite." For example: "If an author managed over a certain number of his pages to produce a feeling of sultriness, or oppression, in the reader, this would unconsciously awaken in the reader the desire for a cold, fresh north wind—and thus some aspect of a north wind would be effective if called forth by some aspect of stuffiness." In "A Game of Chess," after "a desolately low-visioned conversation," the departing drinkers say good night. "And suddenly the poet, feeling his release, drops into another good-night, a good-night with *désinvolture*, a good-night out of what was, within the conditions of the poem at least, a graceful and irrecoverable past." If *désinvolture* means casualness or offhandedness and we relate it to the poet feeling his release, the psychology in the case is first the poet's, and the readers are expected to participate in it: we, too, have had enough of the pub talk and want to be given some other sounds. This privileging of the poet's feelings is unusual in Burke's rhetoric, according to which the reader of a book or the auditor at a play comes first into the reckoning, and the writer is supposed to imagine his or her feelings and gratify them. Burke says that the transition from the good-nights in the public house to Ophelia's good-nights entails "a bold juxtaposition of one quality created by another, an association in ideas which, if not logical, is nevertheless emotionally natural."[5] Imprisoned in one idiom, we find it a relief to be placed in another. The association of one good-night with another is in Eliot's mind, to begin with, and he acts upon it. But Burke does not say how far the association—the juxtaposition—is meant to bring us. Ophelia is deranged, imprisoned in her stray motifs and fantasies. Some of the pathos of her words and gestures may spill over into the characters in the public house: these people are not deranged, but locked in the penury of their gossip and sociality. The good-nights are ordained, it appears, by a rudimentary syntax. The syntax is good enough to make us see one situation in the light of another. That light is the condition of eloquence; the space between the two situations is the space of reverberation.

III

In his own fiction, too, Burke is sensitive to such transitions. Aware that eloquence "is no mere plaster added to a framework of more stable qualities," he starts with language and treats it as if it had all the stable qualities he needs.[6] Considering that his fiction is not well known, I should examine the grounds of his eloquence somewhat historically and biographically.

It is a standard assumption that a writer, having something to say, looks about for the best means of saying it. The some-thing to be said is deemed to come first: it waits around, biting its fingernails, till the writer has found a satisfactory form to express it. Yeats wrote some of his best poems by first knowing, more or less, what he wanted to say. He started by jotting down his thoughts in ordinary, rather commonplace, sentences: later, he revised them, rhyming word with word, into decisive poetry. But that is not always the case. In *Experience into Words* D. W. Harding argued that writers are distinguished from the rest of us by their bringing language—whatever language they are writing in—to bear upon the earliest stage of their cognition; it is as if the words came first and the thoughts, ideas, or imag-inings a split second later. Further: some writers have a gift for certain styles, flourishes, biases of language: the something to be said seems to come later, and is chosen because it enables the particular style to be fulfilled. Presumably, many things such writers might say don't get said because these things don't lend themselves to the choice of style or styles. If a writer has a gift for the jeremiad, he or she is unlikely to write tender passages of love. I do not aspire to Wagnerian amplitudes if my native gift is for the sonata or the *lied*.

In the early months of 1929 Kenneth Burke tried to write a novel along customary lines of plot and character, set in Greenwich Village. The American economy was at that moment taking a crash course in self-destruction, so there was plenty of reality to be apprehended. Conditions were favorable for writing a naturalistic novel in which the hero, a deserving fellow, is defeated by external forces: another *American Tragedy*. Such a novel would require many external details, density of background, an apartment or two, furniture of convincing seediness, bouts of bohemian excess. Burke kept the narrative going as long as he could, but he was disgusted by the result: he threw the typescript away and decided that he must change his procedure. He had written short stories, poems, and essays, but none of these called for the observances of a standard novel. He was devoted to the little magazines, especially to *The Dial*, where editorial inclination favored avant-garde practices. In short: the realistic or naturalistic novel did not allow Burke to use the styles he wanted to use. So he changed his direction, consulting his gifts rather than the public conditions on which they might be employed. He decided that he did not want to deal with external situations; nor was he interested in furniture. He wanted to write passages of "lamentation, rejoicing, beseechment, admonition, sayings, and invective." These seemed to him "central matters, while a plot in which they might occur seemed peripheral, little more than a pretext, justifiable not as a 'good story,' but only insofar as it could bring these six characteristics to the fore." As he said in justifying this decision: "*Facit indignatio versus,* which I should at some risk translate: 'An author may devote his entire energies to rage purely through a preference for long sentences.'"[7]

Burke maintained that his six modes of expression marked, "in a heightened manner, the significant features of each day in our secular, yet somewhat biblical, lives." None of these gestures—lamenting, rejoicing, and so forth—describes the external world or acknowledges it, except indirectly as incentive or provocation. Burke's claim that they mark the significant features of each day in our secular lives is dubious. I spend little energy on any of them. The claim, as I understand it, was Burke's defense against a possible charge of subscribing to "art for art's sake" or Decadence. Each of his six gestures releases an internal motive or capacity, a gift or impulse. Burke beseeches, I infer, not necessarily because he wants anything in particular but because beseeching is one of his favorite styles; he is good at it and therefore likes doing it. Not incidentally but explicitly. He found that "whereas these [six] characteristics can readily be implicit in the realistic, objective novel, one cannot make them explicit, one cannot throw the focus of attention upon them, without continually doing violence to his framework." So he changed his tack. Several of his early writings were on musical themes, and he learned from old-style opera that it was crucial to get fairly quickly to the arias, "whereas the transition from one aria to the next is secondary." The aria delays the drama, but "once the delay is accepted, we may pursue the development of the aria's theme into other aspects of itself."[8]

The logic of Burke's gifts might have suggested that he should commit himself to the essay and write, on Montaigne's authority, essays in each of the six modes. But he evidently thought that he could devise a gnarled form of fiction in which a few rudimentary characters, sketched rather than imagined in depth, would have experiences corresponding to one or more of the six modes of expression. The principle of his conviction is given in a notion he ascribes to John Neal, hero of his *Towards a Better Life:* "If one seeks new metaphors, will he not also find new women?"[9]—a notion which, if valid for metaphor, might facilitate equally fruitful correlations with other figures of thought and speech. This device would enable Burke to practice his gifts as a stylist, one who has "an interest in formal and stylistic twists as such," along with, as a secondary but strong inclination, an interest in "their entanglements in character and plot."[10]

It follows that Burke's sentences must be internally eventful, composed with so much stylistic élan that the absence of objective, newsworthy events passes unnoticed. They are exciting as a good sonnet is, by offering a profusion of verbal events sufficient to engross the most demanding reader. Thus the author hopes to enchant readers who would normally be satisfied only by images of mayhem, and send them back to ordinary life with their lust for excitement somewhat stilled. *Towards a Better Life* and *The Complete White Oxen* are therefore in a strict sense verbal and stylistic, to begin with. Once they are under way, the possibilities of invention are nearly limitless, the figurative resources of the English language being virtually endless. But because words and figures can't be prevented from suggesting forms of life, Burke trades on certain frictions between style and action. In the second chapter of *Towards a Better Life* he has John Neal, twisted as always, making a painful telephone call to his beloved Florence from a public booth: ". . . and while Florence listened to words as desolate as my talent and my predicament could make them, I was grinning into the mouthpiece that the man beyond the glass, waiting to speak here next, might not suspect my condition."[11] Later, at a social gathering of low voltage,

John feels compelled to denounce his rival Anthony in a style of formal complaint: "This ideal is facile and meaningless. . . . You may advocate much, and thus ally yourself with goodness, through being called upon to do nothing. You need face no objective test. Under the guise of giving, you are receiving."

So the story is managed not according to the usual realistic laws of probability but to allow for variety in the sentences. If a certain mood has persisted for a while, it is time for a change. This may seem a puny consideration, but Burke is immensely resourceful in divining when the reader has had enough of a good thing. The essence of stylistic appeal, as he notes in *Permanence and Change,* is ingratiation; gaining favor by saying the right thing. "A plain-spoken people will distrust a man who, bred to different ways of statement, is overly polite and deferential with them, and tends to put his commands in the form of questions (saying 'Would you like to do this' when he means 'Do this')." An example from real alcoholic life:

> I have seen men, themselves schooled in the experiences of alcohol, who knew exactly how to approach a drunken man, bent upon smashing something, and quickly to act upon him by such phrases and intonations as were "just right" for diverting his fluid suggestibility into the channel of maudlin good-fellowship. . . . I should have hated to see a Matthew Arnold tackle the job. He would have been too crude—his training would have been all incapacity.[12]

Eloquence means saying the right, beautiful, possible thing, regardless of consequences. Rhetoric means saying the persuasive thing at the right time to the right person or people, a theorem announced at the end of *Towards a Better Life:* "Speech being a mode of conduct, he converted his faulty living into eloquence. Then should any like his diction, they would indirectly have sanctioned his habits."[13] Sanctioned, not imitated or practiced.

Here is a fairly long passage to show Burke's resourcefulness in making a trope or a formal paradigm develop into an image of life beyond the rhetorical manuals. Think of the movements of a minuet or a choreography of partnering; then think of giving the form an ironic twist:

> Dare I go further among this uneven lot? No further than to mention briefly a beautiful, and even picturesque woman, a Madame Durant, loved by two men. Through letters, telegrams, sudden visits, and the intervention of relatives, she carried her drama tumultuously across many states. With her arms about Joseph, she would cry out that she loved Josephus and thereupon, misled by a desire for too literal a symmetry, would cross the room to embrace Josephus and protest her love of Joseph. For to be alone with one of them seemed far greater impoverishment than to be with neither, and whichever she lived with, she thought herself conscience-stricken for leaving the other, though in reality suffering most from a drop in the liveliness of her situation. She wept in contentment, insisting that she was degraded—and friends, stopping to rebuke her for her inconstancy, would become her suitors. On one occasion I drank a toast to her elopement, using for the purpose glasses given prematurely as a present for her prospective marriage to the groom now temporarily abandoned though on hand to bid her and his rival farewell—and I left in complex cordiality, loving her, her two men, her dog, and

the darkening inhospitable sky which matched my lonesomeness.[14]

We read this prose as if it were poetry, perhaps eighteenth-century couplets in which the outside stays the same while the inside changes from syllable to syllable. Every detail in Madame Durant's emotional life is contained "in principle" in the formal resources of the English language, not forgetting such items as rhyme, alliteration, and assonance. If metaphor suggests a woman, would it not be reasonable to think of human relations equivalent to simile, rhyme, or oxymoron; as we commonly say that a particular situation is ironic, a certain relationship is paradoxical or tragic or comic, moving from tropes to lives without stopping to reflect that that is what we are doing? In the passage I've quoted, Burke's narrator starts out as if he were a disinterested witness or a choreographer of transits—Joseph, Josephus—until we find him a participant in Madame Durant's comings and goings, a victim, a sad sack, committed to loving not only her but her appurtenances, stopping not short of her lovers, her dog, and the sky that overlooks her.

In "The Anaesthetic Revelation of Herone Liddell" Burke has a paragraph that brings these considerations down to one obvious fact, that a word is not the same as the thing or non-thing to which it refers. Herone has been trying to sum things up:

> First, there is man the "economic animal," in the strictly biological sense, such a creature of ecological balance and geophysical necessities as he would be even without his "reason" (that is, without his ability to find words for things and non-things, though frequently, by misuse of his "reason," he puts himself geophysically and ecologically in jeopardy, at the same time victimizing many humble "lower

organisms" that don't quite know what happened to them; but somehow, as the result of human improvising, they ceased to find life lovable, or even livable). Here would prevail, basically, the aims and behaviours that make for growth, self-protection, and reproduction.

Now add *language* (the "grace" that "perfects" nature). Henceforth, every "natural" movement must be complicated by a *linguistic* (or *symbolic*) motive—symbolic not just in the general sense that an animal's posture may be symbolic of its condition, but also in the more specific sense that the word "tree" is symbolic of the thing it names, and this word can undergo developments, such as declensions, syntactic location, grammatical and phonetic changes, that are quite independent of the nature of tree as a thing.[15]

He means the word *tree* in English, of course; *arbre* in French and *albero* in Italian are just as independent of the nature of a tree as English *tree* is, but the possibilities of their development, each within its own language, differ from those of the English *tree*. To enjoy the difference between *tree* and a tree, Herone must love "the sheer jingle of words," and here he finds companionship in Keats's letters: Keats who even in the throes of dying kept on fiddling with words, riding the little horse, summoning up puns for the pleasure of them.

IV

Stevens's most eloquent endings are often achieved by turning upon a particular word, not in anger but in zeal for a last-minute recovery. In "The Snow Man"—his version of Coleridge's "Dejection Ode"—he slides down a long series of murmurings, the repeated words—*sound* and *same*—doing nothing to hold back the slide until the word *nothing* seems to reach the end, a zero of wan wistlessness. But then Stevens lifts the desolating word into a more stirring light:

> For the listener, who listens in the snow,
> And, nothing himself, beholds
> Nothing that is not there and the nothing that is.[16]

Most of the work of transformation is done by the almost parenthetical "nothing himself," which postpones and labors the transition from "the listener, who listens" to "beholds." Halfway through the short poem, Stevens has announced the theme, the "misery" of the sound of the wind in a bare winter landscape and the need to have a mind that can withstand the penury of appearances. When he comes to the near-final *beholds*—another repetition—he seems to be caught in a rigmarole of whisperings and repetitions from which there is no escape. But at the last minute he turns one *nothing* into another, and drives the second one into a new possibility by endowing it with an assertive *is*. What the content of the new *nothing* is, he does not say, except that it is a state redeemed from the old one and added to the vocabulary of Being. We are not to think of it as opulence, a credence of summer, but it is a boon, a blessing.

Sometimes, as in his best short poem, "The Course of a Particular," Stevens effects the recovery a little sooner, just before the end, receiving it with exultation, such that his letting it go doesn't sound like defeat:

> The leaves cry. It is not a cry of divine attention,
> Nor the smoke-drift of puffed-out heroes, nor human
>   cry.
> It is the cry of leaves that do not transcend themselves,

In the absence of fantasia, without meaning more
Than they are in the final finding of the ear, in the thing
Itself, until, at last, the cry concerns no one at all.[17]

It is the claim of the line-ending *thing*, reaching over to the declarative *Itself*, that keeps the poem from being another "Dejection Ode"; it is content to be a response to Shelley's "Ode to the West Wind," though a wintry one. Here, near the end of a long life in post-Romantic poetry, Stevens is prepared to move from the assertion of "the thing/Itself" to a state of feeling close to indifference. He does not now enjoy the privilege of taking the place of God under the name of imagination or the supreme fiction. It is time to let fantasias and the heroics of humanism go. By the time the last line is reached, even though it includes the ominous "at last," we are content to find that the cry concerns "no one at all." The poem, which seemed to divest itself of all its possessions, is formally replete, rich in little acts of change, changing direction syllable by syllable. Stevens has not yet done with phrases: his eloquence is the zest with which he maneuvers among them.

V

It would not be surprising if there were a special kind of eloquence that arose from endings. It might even have a certain sequence. First: a rueful acknowledgment of the privilege of things, Montaigne's "des choses," this, that, and the other, events and entities independent of the words for them. As in Bernard's mind at the end of *The Waves:*

> The clock ticks; the woman sneezes; the waiter comes—there is a gradual coming together, running into one, acceleration and unification. Listen: a whistle sounds, wheels rush, the door creaks on

its hinges. I regain the sense of the complexity and the reality and the struggle, for which I thank you. And with some pity, some envy and much good will, take your hand and bid you good night.[18]

The good-night is implicit in the syntax of its sentence. Every experience is exhausted, but not deleted, in the telling of it, as it is ultimately exhausted by its merely happening. The clock ticks, the woman sneezes. Next: a blessed return to solitude, even if it entails a separation from oneself, perhaps a breakdown.[19] In any event it is a condition in which one sees things disappearing and is content, somewhat like Stevens in "The Course of a Particular," to have them disappear:

> Heaven be praised for solitude! . . . Let me be alone. Let me cast and throw away this veil of being, this cloud that changes with the least breath, night and day, and all night and all day. While I sat here I have been changing. I have watched the sky change. I have seen clouds cover the stars, then free the stars, then cover the stars again. Now I look at their changing no more. Now no one sees me and I change no more. Heaven be praised for solitude that has removed the pressure of the eye, the solicitation of the body, and all need of lies and phrases.

Bernard is talking himself into silence, solitude, the willed bareness of being merely alive, speaking words of one syllable. He has been, from the beginning, an adept of phrases, which like Locke and Husserl but more urbanely he now thinks are lies. In the third part of the sequence, he conjures them away with irony (or thinks he does, but the scene is not yet over):

> What is the phrase for the moon? And the phrase for love? By what name are we to call death? I do

not know. I need a little language such as lovers use, words of one syllable such as children speak when they come into the room and find their mother sewing and pick up some scrap of bright wool, a feather, or a shred of chintz. I need a howl; a cry. When the storm crosses the marsh and sweeps over me where I lie in the ditch unregarded I need no words. Nothing neat. Nothing that comes down with all its feet on the floor. None of those reso-nances and lovely echoes that break and chime from nerve to nerve in our breasts, making wild music, false phrases. I have done with phrases.

How much better is silence; the coffee-cup, the table. How much better to sit by myself like the solitary sea-bird that opens its wings on the stake. Let me sit here for ever with bare things, this coffee-cup, this knife, this fork, things in them-selves, myself being myself.

It is the gratification of being nothing but at last one's self, having the same bare mode of existence as a coffee cup. The trouble is that a coffee cup doesn't want any more, it is complete, it has achieved its plenitude. We haven't, so we want more; even Bernard does. But this passage enacts his determined reduction of himself to the least form of life consistent with its being life at all: children, howls, cries, syllables. It is a desperate claim upon penury. In the next phase he must drag himself up and go out to the world, the dawn, the whitening sky, "some sort of renewal":

A redness gathers on the roses, even on the pale rose that hangs by the bedroom window. A bird chirps. Cottagers light their early candles. Yes, this is the eternal renewal, the incessant rise and fall and fall and rise again.

Bernard, too, is swept up into the rhythm of it. Though he has done with phrases, he cannot be done with figures. In the last part of the sequence he confronts death, the sole remaining enemy:

> And in me too the wave rises. It swells; it arches its back. I am aware once more of a new desire, something rising beneath me like the proud horse whose rider first spurs and then pulls him back. What enemy do we now perceive advancing against us, you whom I ride now, as we stand pawing this stretch of pavement? It is death. Death is the enemy. It is death against whom I ride with my spear couched and my hair flying back like a young man's, like Percival's, when he galloped in India. I strike spurs into my horse. Against you I will fling myself, unvanquished and unyielding, O Death![20]

He is still making phrases; he could not live without figures, metaphors, personifications, the doomed chivalry of speech. His eloquence at the end—only the waves have the last word, "*The waves broke on the shore*"—is archaic, hopeless—"my spear couched"—invoking the gone England of Shakespeare's history plays in his zeal to fight those waves, like Yeats's Cuchulain. No rhetoric is entailed. Bernard is not speaking to anyone: no palpable aim is in view. The force of his speech is entirely inward, self-dramatizing in a little play entirely his own, a play of himself and Death, a lyric drama more inward than *Krapp's Last Tape*.

The passages I have quoted from *The Waves* traverse the most notable forms of eloquence. First: phrases, Bernard's word for the high style, perhaps the sublime, the furthest reach of expression within the poor limits of language. Next: little language. The most famous "little language" in English is Swift's *Journal to Stella*, which I think is in Bernard's mind, baby talk, ideally syllables before they have suffered the fate or realized the destiny of joining with other syllables to become words. Another example, just as famous, is Lear to Cordelia in the British camp near Dover, when he refuses to see Goneril and Regan and, instead, lisps to Cordelia a vision of their fellowship in prison, as in a condition of a redeemed nature freed from culture:

> No, no, no, no! Come, let's away to prison:
> We two alone will sing like birds i' th' cage:
> When thou dost ask me blessing, I'll kneel down,
> And ask of thee forgiveness: so we'll live,
> And pray, and sing, and tell old tales, and laugh
> At gilded butterflies, and hear poor rogues
> Talk of court news; and we'll talk with them too,
> Who loses and who wins; who's in, who's out;
> And take upon's the mystery of things,
> As if we were God's spies: and we'll wear out,
> In a wall'd prison, packs and sects of great ones,
> That ebb and flow by th' moon.
> *(5.3.8–18)*

It is all game, child's play, even the kneeling down and the forgiveness, the reduction of large news to gossip, it is all "as if." The second-last phase of Bernard's self-communing is the one in which he comes back again to respect the bare eloquence by which a coffee cup is a coffee cup, itself without transcendence or fantasia. In his fantasy of jousting with Death—pale horse, pale rider—he has nothing to keep him on horseback but words.

6

Blind Mouths

I

I have been saying that some distinctive forms of eloquence arise at the end; the end of a life or a phase of life, the end of a story. Especially distraught kinds of eloquence issue from a mind at the end of its tether. Or from a mind, still resilient enough, facing the objective lapse of its resources or coming to an outer limit of the medium it is using or being used by—as in dream, vision, prophecy, and mystical trance. Daniel's vision of "a certain man clothed in linen" ends with an admonition to silence:

> And I heard the man clothed in linen, which *was* upon the waters of the river, when he held up his right hand and his left and unto heaven, and sware by him that liveth for ever that *it shall be* for a time, times, and an half; and when he shall have accomplished to scatter the power of the holy people, all these *things* shall be finished.
>
> And I heard, but I understood not: then said I, O my Lord, what *shall* be the end of these *things?*
>
> And he said, Go thy way Daniel: for the words *are* closed up and sealed till the time of the end. (Dan. 12:7–9)

It is hard to read that passage without hovering upon the eloquence of "a time, times, and an half," before proceeding to the end in silence. It is different with the fraught Psalmist, caught between praise of the Lord and execration of His enemies, who takes a breath of release from both duties and cries out, "Though ye have lien among the pots, yet shall ye be as the wings of a dove covered with silver, and her feathers with yellow gold" (68:13). It is as if the language intervened to save him by eloquence. The pathos incited by evidence of limits and endings is understandable, even if there is satisfaction meanwhile in the work accomplished. One wants to go on forever working with one's instruments and finding them adequate to one's ambition. Often they are not.

There is a trivial side to this sense of an ending. Charles Rosen has remarked that "a musical system has important attributes of a language, like grammar and syntax, although some of the aspects of communication are very rudimentary—that is, you can convey emotion with music, and imitate cuckoos and babbling brooks, but you cannot make a dinner appointment or a train reservation without words."[1] Serious composers don't worry about that restriction. But they worry when they sense the possibility of something creative that might be done and it turns out that they can't do it in music because music-as-such, however eloquent in its own ways, won't allow it. There are minds that thrive on such exigency, and it may be that every mind should assume a categorical lack, destitution, or failure in the experience it engages. Most composers seem content with their instruments, but maybe they should have a sense of disaster beyond their endowments. T. W. Adorno said of the philosopher Ernst Bloch that he had "an exaggerated passion for the possibility lying defeated, as impossibility, in the midst of reality." Why the passion was an exaggerated one, Adorno does not say. "Like all thought worthy of the name, Bloch's thrives on the edge of failure, in close proximity to sympathy for the occult."[2] The occult is beyond reason and syntax.

There is a passage in the first canto of the *Paradiso* in which Dante, gazing at Beatrice, who is gazing at the sun, speaks of an experience that lies beyond the human scale and in the same breath says that it is impossible to speak of such a thing: "Trasumanar significar *per verba*/non si poria"—The passing beyond the human [state] cannot be indicated in words:

> Nel suo aspetto tal dentro mi fei,
> qual si fé Glauco nel gustar de l'erba
> che 'l fé consorto in mar de li altri dèi.
> Trasumanar significar *per verba*
> non si poria; però l'essemplo basti
> a cui esperïenza grazia serba.[3]

Glaucon, according to Ovid's *Metamorphoses* (XIII.906–65), was a fisherman who sat down one day on a grassy spot where no one had ever been before, to count his catch.[4] The fish began to slither about on the grass and made their way back to the sea. Thinking that this must be due to some property in the grass, Glaucon chewed some leaves of it and immediately began to yearn for the ocean. He plunged into the sea and was changed into a sea god by Oceanus and Tethys. Dante says that no such transformation is possible for him: his form of it will have to come from a divine power. As if to mime the impossibility, he swerves from his otherwise capable Italian into a Latin more erudite in its sense of that intuition. In the twelfth and thirteenth centuries, as Hugh Kenner has noted, Latin was the encoding medium for the gravest topics available to anyone's mind: "God's word, men's most intricate reflections on God's word, and the analytic tools by which thought acts on thought itself."[5] Dante also has in view St. Paul's account, in the second letter to the Corinthians, of a man ("whether in the body or out of the body, I cannot tell; God knoweth") who was "caught up into paradise, and heard unspeakable words, which it is not lawful for a man to utter" (2 Cor. 12:4). In *per verba* Dante invokes the tradition in which the meaning of the episode in Corinthians has been pondered, mainly by Augustine and Aquinas. These are his chief authorities on the relation between human experience and that outer limit of it which testifies, however inadequately, to a vision of God. In the letter to Can Grande della Scala, Dante refers to the same passage in Corinthians and draws from it the same lesson, that the human mind may reach such a state of exaltation that, after it returns to its normal condition, its memory fails, since it has transcended the range of human faculty *(propter transcendisse humanum modum).* Dante is "transhumanized," already turned toward the divine vision, but he cannot express such an experience in words, Italian or Latin. The same lesson is recited from Matthew and from Ezekiel. In the letter to Can Grande, Dante points to the limitation of language:

> For we see many things with the intellect for which there are no verbal signs. This fact Plato makes plain enough by the use he makes of metaphors in his books: for he saw many things by the light of the intellect which he was unable to express in the appropriate words.[6]

Dante's phrase—*sermone proprio*—leaves open the question: did Plato succeed in expressing "everything" by recourse to metaphors, or was there a realm of the intellect that had to remain unspoken, even with figures at hand? In canzone 2 of the *Convito* Dante seems to lay equal blame for the deficiencies of his poetry on the weakness of his understanding and the inadequacies of Italian. Already in the fourth century, Hilary of Poitiers had written that the mystery of the Trinity was "beyond the denotative power of speech, beyond the representative power of sense, beyond the conceptual power of the senses": *Extra*

significantiam sermonis est, extra sensus intentionem, extra intelli-
gentiae conceptionem.[7]

These questions are pondered in Latin because Latin is wiser than the vernacular languages in the apprehension of spiritual experience. It may be suggested that the point is invalidated by the *De Vulgari Eloquentiae*, because there Dante seems to say that Italian is older than Latin and more intimately responsive to the original experience of God's presence. Dante's idea is that Adam's language was Hebrew and that the modern European languages emerged from Hebrew as three linguistic families. According to this idea, Latin was an artificial language, deliberately constructed in conventional, changeless terms so that our common knowledge of distant times and peoples would be preserved. Latin was never, in Dante's view, a native or mother tongue. But the point is not invalidated. Apart from the fact that Dante's ideas on the origin of languages as outlined in the *De Vulgari Eloquentiae* are virtually repudiated in the *Divina Commedia*, there is a clear recognition that Latin, whether older or younger than the vernacular languages, is the language in which the relation between experience and speech has been most fully examined. The stability of the Latin of Augustine and Aquinas is invoked in debating such questions as the speech of God, Adam's speech, the building of Babel, the confusion of tongues. In the passage from the *Paradiso*, Dante is pointing toward a kind of experience for which an impossibly pure and rarefied language would be required, such as the speech of angels. The effect of *per verba* is to lead the mind beyond its vernacular concerns toward a form of speech neither Latin nor Italian but the original language before Babel in which, we assume, any experience could be expressed.

Dante's tone in this passage is not rueful or dispirited. Seeing Beatrice, he apprehends supernatural grace, and knows that he, too, is moving up toward the divine vision. Some minds, content with their positivism, want to believe that there is nothing but nature—we have nothing but phenomena—and they speak of esoteric divinations with contempt. They don't want to know, if knowledge is to be of that kind: they regard the expressive limits they meet as merely in the course of things. But the existence of figures of speech and thought is enough to show that even positivists are not always content merely to transcribe the given facts *in proprio sermone*. Dante exults to come to the end of ordinary speech, because the next phase of experience is at hand and it hardly matters to him that there are no words for it.

A limit of another kind—with its appropriate eloquence—is reached at the end of canto 26 of *Purgatorio,* where Dante hastens to speak to Arnaut Daniel. What Arnaut says is given in his own language, Provençal. If it were given in Dante's Italian, it would have to be in reported speech. The lines ascribed to Arnaut are a supreme compliment by which one master allows another ("miglior fabbro del parlar materno") to speak in his own tongue—or in that tongue as Dante imagines it—rather than suffer the indignity of a swift assimilation into Italian, where his voice would be heard only at one remove:

> "Tan m'abellis vostre cortes deman,
> qu'ieu no me puesc ni voill a vos cobrire.
>
> Ieu sui Arnaut, que plor e vau cantan;
> consiros vei la passada folor,
> e vei jausen lo joi qu'esper, denan.
>
> Ara vos prec, per aquella valor
> que vos guida al som d l'escalina,
> sovenha vos a temps de ma dolor!"[8]

The eloquence of this speech arises from its delivering, through Dante's sympathetic imagination, Arnaut's last words. Only one line of Dante's narrative in this canto succeeds them: "Poi s'ascose nel foco che li affina"—He then hid himself in the refining flame. T. S. Eliot said that "the really fine rhetoric of Shakespeare occurs in situations where a character in the play *sees himself* in a dramatic light," citing examples from *Othello, Coriolanus,* and *Timon of Athens.*[9] There is no light more dramatic than the one in which we face our death, or, in Arnaut's case, his transformation into a new state. Another aspect of this eloquence is the concentration of an entire life into a line, a sentence: "Ieu sui Arnaut, que plor e vau cantan"—I am Arnaut, who weeps and goes singing. The next lines distribute the tears and the song:

> consiros vei la passada folor,
> e vei jausen lo joi qu'esper, denan.

"In tears I see my past folly, and joyously I see before me the joy that I await." "Ara vos prec . . ."—Now I pray you, by that power which guides you to the top of this stairway, while it is yet time, be mindful of my pain! It is a mark of Dante's delicacy—and of the eloquence that results—that he effects internal rhyme and end rhyme from the standard words of Provençal love poetry *(plor, folor, valor, dolor)* while providing a context that points every conventional word toward another meaning, higher or lower. *Folor* does not mean local folly but a lifetime given to lust. *Valor* means the power of God, not of man or woman. *Dolor* is not a lover's pain of passion but the passion of a degraded lifetime.[10] Only the tears, *plor,* remain the same, in kind if not in degree.

It is a complication, but an enabling one, that we are likely to hear the lines that Dante has assigned to Arnaut with echoes and repetitions of them in modern poetry: "Sovegna vos" in Eliot's "Ash-Wednesday," *Ara Vos Prec* (1919), Eliot's book of poems, and "consiros," which ends a line in Pound's canto 83 that began with a reference to Yeats's "Down by the Salley Gardens," ". . . and now am full of tears." Full of tears, *consiros*.[11]

There is another instance of the "eloquence of the end" in the *Inferno*, canto 31. Virgil and Dante are crossing the broad bank between the tenth *bolgia* and the central pit of Hell. They see, looming through the dusk, the forms of giants, as large as towers. The named ones are Nimrod, Ephialtes, Briareus, and Antaeus—all, except Antaeus, damned for their pride in trying to scale Heaven. We learn from Genesis, chapters 6, 10, and 11, that "Cush begat Nimrod," who became a great hunter and a giant":

> And the whole earth was of one language, and of one speech.
>
> And it came to pass, as they journeyed from the east, that they found a plain in the land of Shi-nar; and they dwelt there.
>
> And they said one to another, Go to, let us make brick, and burn them thoroughly. And they had brick for stone, and slime had they for mortar.
>
> And they said, Go to, let us build a city and a tower, whose top may reach unto heaven; and let us make us a name, lest we be scattered abroad upon the face of the whole earth.
>
> And the LORD came down to see the city and the tower, which the children of men builded.
>
> And the LORD said, Behold, the people *is* one, and they have all one language; and this they begin to do: and now nothing will be restrained from them, which they have imagined to do.
>
> Go to, let us go down, and there confound their language, that they may not understand one another's speech.

> So the LORD scattered them abroad from thence upon the face of all the earth: and they left off to build the city.
>
> Therefore is the name of it called Babel; because the LORD did there confound the language of all the earth: and from thence did the LORD scatter them abroad upon the face of all the earth. (Gen. 11:1–9)

As Virgil and Dante pass by, Nimrod shouts: *"Raphèl maì amècche zabì almi."* It is gibberish: no scholar has ever made sense of it, but—for all one knows—it might be commensurate to the "matter and impertinency mixed, reason in madness" of King Lear. Virgil rounds on Nimrod: "You imbecile soul, take your horn and use it, if you must relieve your anger or any other passion. Search around your neck, you confused soul, and you will find the rope that holds it fast. The horn is curved across your massive chest." Then Virgil says to Dante: "Elli stessi s'accusa": He accuses himself.

Whatever Nimrod's words mean to him, there is no evidence that they intend self-accusation. The sinner *"per lo cui mal co-to/pur un linguaggio nel mondo non s'usa"* (through whose ill thought the world does not use one language only) could shout a justification of his actions by appealing to an extreme nationalism of sentiment. The fact that the appeal would be incommunicable would point not to a defect in his program or even to an error of method but merely to consequences beyond his intention. It is absurd that Virgil denounces Nimrod and tells him in strict Italian that the only instrument of expression he has is the hunter's horn on his chest—in Italian, a language that by definition Nimrod can't understand any better than Virgil can understand Nimrod's idiolect. I assume that Nimrod's outburst was enforced by gestures of frustration and ferocity that make a universal language understandable by anyone without the words. When Othello comes ranting to Desdemona in act 4, scene 2, with words as foreign to her as Nimrod's to Virgil or Virgil's to Nimrod, she answers: "I understand a fury in your words, / But not the words."

II

Is it to gain a nuance of eloquence that, speaking English—or at least some idiolect of English—we bring in a word or phrase from another language? Why do we so casually say *status quo, vice versa, jeux d'esprit, je ne sais quoi, joie de vivre, Zeitgeist, sole meunière, volte face, sotto voce*? In one issue of the *New York Review of Books* I find *jus ad bellum, jus in bello, horror vacui, flora* and *fauna, tour de force, ad infinitum, pace,* and *détente.* Why use foreign phrases to describe movements in music, ballet, and ice skating but not in theater? In "Fragment of an Analysis of a Case of Hysteria" Freud breaks into French when he wants to enforce an attitude of intelligent worldliness in sexual matters. Luther's table talk shows that he regularly switched from German to Latin when the theme became severely intellectual or theological. In the fourth section of "Ash Wednesday," "Sovegna vos" has no discursive relation to the lines that precede it, "Made cool the dry rock and made firm the sand" and "In blue of larkspur, blue of Mary's colour," so for justification we must go back to the implied speaker, and give his or her interior monologue absolute privilege. The movement through the lines is an example of "qualitative progression," in Kenneth Burke's phrase, where one thing, one line leads to the next not by rational necessity as in an argument but by right of association in the implied speaker's mind. If "Sovegna vos" occurred to Eliot (let us call him the speaker) at that moment in relation to everything that had preceded it, then we can have no complaint, he is for the moment the master, the "miglior fabbro." At the end of *The Waste Land*, we read: "*Le Prince d'Aquitaine à la tour abolie.*" The only reason for this line is that it is one of the fragments the speaker has shored against his ruins. The prince has not otherwise appeared in the poem. "Why then Ile fit you. Hieronymo's mad againe" is part of a line spoken by Hieronimo in Kyd's *The Spanish Tragedy*, followed by the subtitle of that play. Apart from the tenuous consideration that the murderers who act in the entertainment that Hieronimo is to put on must each speak "in unknown languages," "that it may breed the more variety," the line has no bearing on *The Waste Land* except that it evidently inhabits Eliot's mind and memory. We take the poet's word for the words he quotes and those he speaks on his own authority. What we make of them is our own choice. We are also free to think of "the speaker" as a person who might be met outside the poem, or as an ontologically vague or mobile entity, or indeed as a mere grammatical subject. Who is the real Julius Caesar? For the time being, in the last lines of *The Waste Land*, the "I" is merely what Hugh Kenner called a "zone of consciousness" in which certain verbal events take place. The quotations are such events.

But quotations are not docile. Walter Benjamin said that "quotations in my work are like wayside robbers who leap out armed and relieve the stroller of his conviction."[12] At least they relieve him of the conviction that his is the only mind that needs to be listened to. "When you write at any serious pitch of obligation," Geoffrey Hill has maintained, "you enter into the nature of grammar and etymology which is a nature contrary to your own." One should not assume "the concurrence of language with one's expectations."[13] Facile instances of eloquence arise from this assumption, as if to say: if I have done the language the honor of speaking it, should it not return the favor by expressing my sole self? A quotation impedes this familiarity by being a special case of language in its estranging disposition: it holds out against being assimilated to one's intention. Hill therefore calls a language "enemy country." Hence the value of foreign words, at least until they have been domesticated, their foreignness forgotten. *Joie de vivre* is no longer foreign, we have nearly forgotten that it was once a recent French import. Adorno has argued that we should not demonstrate the harmlessness of foreign words, but rather try to release their explosive force; as Rilke used them in *Neue Gedichte* "to call by their proper names objects that are rejected, faded, and petrified, and to awaken them abruptly in the echo they send back: 'Du schnell vergehendes Daguerreotyp/in meinen langsamer vergehenden Händen' ('You quickly fading daguerreotype in my more slowly fading hands')." Foreign words have their legitimacy "as an expression of alienation itself" and for the hope they bring that human beings may someday be released from their imprisonment in "preconceived language." The worst position to take, according to Adorno, is to think of a language as having an organic development, issuing from nature and myth, such that every word will be authenticated by having emerged as night from day. In Genesis, God did not reveal the names of things to man. Those names were made known to him only in Adam's naming them "in his human fashion." In each act of naming, "genius escapes anew from mythic bondage."[14] Honorable eloquence is not a gratuity we receive for services rendered to our native language, gestures of piety we perform in its favor. It is won from the language by acts of naming, adumbrating, and performing—often despite what a "natural" affection for the language would suggest. It is speech against the grain.

It follows that the only forms of eloquence acceptable to Adorno—and to Benjamin, and later to Paul de Man—are those that emerge from catastrophe; they are found in allegory rather than symbolism, in Surrealism rather than Impressionism. In Adorno's case, Schoenberg's eloquence, and Berg's, and Webern's are to be praised, not Stravinsky's. Benjamin writes:

> Whereas in the symbol destruction is idealized and the transfigured face of nature is fleetingly revealed in the light of redemption, in allegory the observer is confronted with the *facies hippocratica* of history as a petrified, primordial landscape. Everything about history that, from the very beginning, has been untimely, sorrowful, unsuccessful, is expressed in a face—or rather in a death's head.[15]

The death's head is even more eloquently invoked in Benjamin's *One-Way Street:*

> The incomparable language of the death's head: total expressionlessness—the black of the eye-sockets—coupled to the most unbridled expression—the grinning rows of teeth.[16]

But those teeth only appear to be grinning, and appear so to Benjamin alone.

III

If you feel impelled to reject the gift of symbols—the apparently easy accord by which a symbol "is always a part of the totality that it represents" (in de Man's formulation) you will move toward irony and allegory, where no such gratification is on offer.[17] If, further, you feel impelled not simply to take grim dictation from allegory and sad wisdom from irony but to do the best you can for eloquence, even in such hard conditions, you may feel inclined to seize a wild property of language and make it your own; indeed, make it yourself. The particular excess that is especially to the point is catachresis, the wrenching of language from the propriety of its normal reference. The rhetorical treatises call it "the figure of abuse"; it carries an implication of wrongdoing among the words even when, in the end, it turns mischief into good. Hamlet speaks of taking up arms "against a sea of troubles." Milton's Hell in book 1 of *Paradise Lost* shows "no light, but rather darkness visible." If you revered decorum above all, you would call these lines abusive. Every instance of oxymoron would come up for the same description, if you took logic to heart. Locke considers catachresis in the third book of his *Essay Concerning Human Understanding* without calling it by that name: he describes it as an abuse of words by which we posit anything we like and think that our words denote real things. He speaks of it as if it were an error most of us fall into through naïveté or negligence: "He that thinks the name *centaur* stands for some real being, imposes on himself and mistakes words for things."[18] But you could think that *centaur* stands for some real being and be innocently in error—you just got it wrong, and you hardly deserve to be scolded by Locke for it. Catachresis could also be a deliberate act by which we use the word *centaur*, perhaps in the phrase *a flute-playing centaur*, without being wrong about it: we might have it stand for an imaginary being, and have a use for it in that imagining. It might be mainly a rather desperate attempt to impose one's will on the language. In the lines from "The Second Coming" that I've looked at in an earlier chapter, Yeats imagines "a shape with lion body and the head of a man, / A gaze blank and pitiless as the sun." Such a thing doesn't exist—nor does Yeats think it does, any more than Picasso thought that women had two eyes on the same side of their faces—but he imagines that it might come into existence, as a child in a rocking cradle came into the world with equally startling effect to give the present age its name.

Locke would have no time for these imaginings. He thought that language had only one reason to exist, to represent the ideas in our minds. Reviewing the several forms of abuse of words, he held that "by constant and familiar use" such mistaken use of words for things charmed people "into notions far remote from the truth of things."[19] His sense of "the truth of things" was penurious, he did not willingly allow that the imagination left to its freedom might be engaged in serious business and serious play. He did not want to talk about language, he regarded the whole subject as a nuisance, though unavoidable. The thought that a creative sense of language might entail using it intrinsically or experimentally would have appalled him: he would have denounced such practices as sophistry. But the sophists, too, had a justifiably catachrestic way with words and eloquence, as E. M. Cioran argues:

> Inured to a purely verbal art of thinking, the sophists were the first to occupy themselves with a meditation upon words, their value, propriety, and function in the conduct of reasoning: the capital step toward the discovery of style, conceived as a goal in itself, as an intrinsic end, was taken. It merely remained to transpose this verbal quest, to assign as its object: the harmony of the sentence, to substitute for the play of abstraction the play of expression. The artist reflecting on his means is therefore indebted to the sophist and organically related to him. Both pursue, in different directions, the same genre of activity. Having ceased to be *nature,* they live as a function of the word. "Reality" is not [the sophist's] concern: he knows it depends on the signs which express it and which must, simply, be mastered.[20]

Catachresis is one sign of mastery: its use is possible, and therefore desirable as a rejection of the servitude that Locke tried to impose on speech and writing. In Baudelaire's *De l'essence du rire* laughter and caricature are catachreses, they vehemently swerve from normal behavior and know what they are about. And while we think of catachreses as local acts of violence in language, there are entire works which are catachreses on principle, such as *Finnegans Wake* and the Alice books. Swift is catachrestic in *A Tale of a Tub* when he makes it impossible for us to know who is speaking at a given moment or how to ascribe any source to the words other than a printing press. There is a frantic element in these books, as in Kafka's *Metamorphosis*, making their joy a grim sensation, in part because catastrophe has overwhelmed the ostensibly genial relations between man and nature, individuals and society, experience and civility.

Handbooks of rhetoric regularly cite passages in *Macbeth* and "Lycidas" as instances of catachresis. When Macbeth is backing out of the plan to kill Duncan—"We will proceed no further in this business"—his wife rounds upon him:

> Was the hope drunk
> Wherein you dress'd yourself? Hath it slept since?
> And wakes it now, to look so green and pale
> At what it did so freely?
> *(1.7.35–38)*

It looks like an ordinary mixed metaphor. Were you drunk, not in your right mind, when you wrote to me of your ambition? When you imagined yourself dressed in royal robes? Was your ambition drunk when you dressed yourself earlier today? The effect of the alliteration (*drunk* at the end of the line and *dress'd* dominating the next one) is to override the oddity and make the question seem unanswerable. Macbeth has put the image of noble garments into his wife's mind:

> . . . and I have bought
> Golden opinions from all sorts of people,
> Which would be worn now in their newest gloss,
> Not cast aside so soon.
> *(1.7.32–35)*

She hailed him as "Glamis" and "Cawdor": maybe he should be
happy to show off those honors for a while before reaching for
the gold. Lady Macbeth brushes these small rewards aside. She
has identified him with his ambition—"the hope"—and now
that he has sobered up, he has turned coward. Her first question
to him is a catachresis, her rage drives through the distinctions
that a more equable person would make. When a catachresis
is eloquent—it isn't always—we feel the pressure of the values
the speaker doesn't care about. She should care about them,
and would on another occasion, but she can't stop to care now.
What she should observe is decorum, which should extend
itself all the way and fend off every affront to it. But a mind at
the end of its tether can't be expected to be decorous.

One of the most peremptory catachreses in English comes in
"Lycidas" when St. Peter denounces false shepherds, the bish-
ops:

> Last came, and last did go,
> The Pilot of the *Galilean* lake,
> Two massy Keyes he bore of metals twain,
> (The Golden opes, the Iron shuts amain)
> He shook his Miter'd locks, and stern bespake,
> How well could I have spar'd for thee, young swain,
> Anow of such as for their bellies sake,
> Creep and intrude, and climb into the fold?
> Of other care they little reck'ning make,
> Then how to scramble at the shearers feast,
> And shove away the worthy bidden guest;

Blind mouthes! that scarce themselves know how to
   hold
A Sheep-hook, or have learn'd ought els the least
That to the faithfull Herdsmans art belongs!
What recks it them? What need they? They are sped;
And when they list, their lean and flashy songs
Grate on their scrannel Pipes of wretched straw,
The hungry Sheep look up, and are not fed,
But swoln with wind, and the rank mist they draw,
Rot inwardly, and foul contagion spread:
Besides what the grim Woolf with privy paw
Daily devours apace, and nothing sed,
But that two-handed engine at the door,
Stands ready to smite once, and smite no more.[21]

The hungry sheep look up to be fed, but all they get is more
words, rigmaroles: *swoln* needs to have *swelling* nearby as a term
of bombastic style. This is a minor catachresis. But the bold
one is "Blind mouthes!" The speech puts the elegiac tone of
"Lycidas" under strain, but no more so than one of its models,
Peter's attack on the corrupt election of Pope Boniface VIII, as
given in book 27 of Dante's *Paradiso*, where it might be thought
to cloud the visionary atmosphere at the end of the poem. In
any case, Milton's Peter has behind him not only Dante but
the corrupt shepherds in Ezekiel, Christ's parable of the Good
Shepherd, and the keys of the kingdom in Matthew. It was
Ruskin who first, so far as I know, drew attention to the oddity
of "Blind mouthes!" and explained its propriety:

> I pause again, for this is a strange expression; a bro-
> ken metaphor, one might think, careless and un-
> scholarly.
>
>   Not so: its very audacity and pithiness are in-
> tended to make us look close at the phrase and re-

member it. Those two monosyllables express the precisely accurate contraries of right character, in the two great offices of the Church—those of bishop and pastor.

A Bishop means a person who sees.

A Pastor means one who feeds.

The most unbishoply character a man can have is therefore to be Blind.

The most unpastoral is, instead of feeding, to want to be fed,—to be a Mouth.

Take the two reverses together, and you have "blind mouths."[22]

Very true. But to bring about his conclusion, Ruskin has to prise the two words apart and think of them separately, as if they were both nouns rather than the first an adjective qualifying the second, a noun. It is only when you have put them together again, in due grammatical relation, that you see how strange the phrase is. You might find yourself thinking of certain mouths in paintings by Munch, de Chirico, and Francis Bacon for comparison. And trying to think of "mouths" simultaneously as gluttons and as windbags. The eloquence is a striking excess of saying, such that no single statement is fully made.

IV

My theme in this chapter has been the particular forms of eloquence that are available somewhat desperately and nailbitingly at the outer limit of a language; available to minds that sense that there are further things that might be glimpsed, even if it's unlikely that they can be known or expressed. The theme is a weak version of Empson's argument, in "This Last Pain," that you can live decently even if you have no belief to act on or appeal to. A weak version, because the stakes are not at all as high: they touch on achieving yet another form of eloquence; that's all but it isn't nothing. Here are the two last stanzas of Empson's poem:

> Feign then what's by a decent tact believed
> And act that state is only so conceived,
>   And build an edifice of form
>   For house where phantoms may keep warm.
>
> Imagine, then, by miracle, with me,
> (Ambiguous gifts, as what gods give must be)
>   What could not possibly be there,
>   And learn a style from a despair.[23]

In an earlier stanza, Empson refers to Wittgenstein's claim that "a thought contains the possibility of the situation of which it is a thought: what is thinkable is possible too."[24] That seems not to be true: there are many paintings, some poems, and some sentences that do not correspond to a "situation" in any world we know or can conceive. To make the claim feasible, we should have to give a shadowy meaning to *possible* and *possibility*. "An edifice of form" would house such figments. "And learn a style from a despair." That is much more feasible: it's what I have been talking about. Empson's poetic "style" is a particular way of being in the world; so is any style. "A despair" is his phrase for the agnostic predicament he thinks inevitable among decent people: they have to live with it, one way or another. In language, it means being on the edge and achieving whatever eloquence you can by being there. Empson may have a more pointed reference in view. In *Either/Or* Kierkegaard says that "when the age loses the tragic, it gains despair."[25] Despair: a term we might add to those we have already met—irony, allegory, the *Trauerspiel* that Benjamin studied. But most of the eloquence is in *feign,* the resoluteness of its being the first word in the line, the rueful settling in *then* for the best that can be managed, the subdued claim in *decent,* the refusal to claim too much in *tact,* the honorableness of saying *believed* when we know very well that the true sentiment is far less than belief.

7

For and Against

Over, over, there is a soft place in my heart for all that is over, no, for the being over, I love the word, words have been my only loves, not many.
— Samuel Beckett, *"From an Abandoned Work"*

There are also certain rules of the more flamboyant discipline now called eloquence, which are valid in spite of the fact that they can be used to commend falsehood.
— *Augustine,* De Doctrina Christiana

I

The most forceful rejection of eloquence I am aware of is Christ's: "Get thee behind me, Satan," an admonition extended in the Sermon on the Mount (Matt. 4 and 5) to an ethic recommending the plain style, plain dealing, humility, truth, and justice. But Christ must have been in some degree of thrall to Satan's eloquence, "being forty days tempted of the devil," as Luke reports (4:2), and submitting himself to it in "the holy city" and on "an exceeding high mountain," before casting him aside: "Then saith Jesus unto him, 'Get thee hence, Satan.'" Matthew and Luke dispose of the episode in a few verses. All they tell us is that Satan tempted Christ to exert his power and offered him the whole world "if thou wilt fall down and worship me."

In *Paradise Regained*, Milton imagines more detail, starting with God's decision to have His son engage with Satan and

143

overcome him. Christ does not renounce the standard proce-
dures of rhetoric. He intends

> By winning words to conquer willing hearts,
> And make persuasion do the work of fear.
> *(1: 222–23)*[1]

When Satan appears in the guise of "an aged man in Rural
weeds," Christ recognizes him and calls him a liar:

> That hath been thy craft,
> By mixing somewhat true to vent more lies.
> *(1.432–33)*

He also warns him that

> henceforth Oracles are ceast,
> And thou no more with Pomp and Sacrifice
> Shalt be inquir'd at *Delphos* or elsewhere.
> *(1: 456–58)*

But Satan continues to tempt Christ with offers of food and
drink, wealth, glory, power, the throne of David, Tiberius's
Rome, Jerusalem, and the contemplative treasures of Athens,
its knowledge, wisdom, learning, and philosophy—

> *Athens,* the eye of *Greece,* Mother of Arts
> And Eloquence . . .
> *(4: 240–41)*

The offers include the treasures of Plato, Aristotle, Zeno, Pin-
dar, Homer, the tragic dramatists, and the orators:

> Thence to the famous Orators repair,
> Those ancient, whose resistless eloquence
> Wielded at will that fierce Democracy . . .
> *(4: 267–69)*

Christ, unmoved by these big names, also dismisses the philosophies of Pyrrho, Epicurus, and the Stoics in favor of the dear feast of Hebrew and the Psalms:

> Remove their swelling Epithets thick laid
> As varnish on a Harlot's cheek, the rest,
> Thin sown with aught of profit or delight,
> Will far be found unworthy to compare
> With *Sion's* songs, to all true tastes excelling,
> Where God is prais'd aright, and Godlike men,
> The Holiest of Holies, and his Saints . . .
> *(4: 343–49)*

The orators are rejected by comparison with the prophets:

> Thir Orators thou then extoll'st, as those
> The top of Eloquence, Statists indeed,
> And lovers of thir Country, as may seem;
> But herein to our Prophets far beneath,
> As men divinely taught, and better teaching
> The solid rules of Civil Government
> In thir majestic unaffected style
> Than all the Oratory of *Greece* and *Rome.*
> *(4: 353–60)*

At this point, and not before time, Satan gives up trying to persuade Christ and instead resorts to thunder, lightning, and nightmares.

II

Since the Gospels and Paul's epistles—though not solely because of them—it has become harder to make a case for eloquence than against it. The Sermon on the Mount established the decorum to be observed: straight talk (though some matters might be kept secret among one's apostles and disciples). In a sermon of 1623 on the Penitential Psalms, Donne invoked no less an authority than the Holy Ghost to prescribe the mean or middle style, though it was a style hospitable to figures of speech and thought:

> And first give me leave by the way, only in passing, by occasion of those words which are here rendred, *Convertentur, &* Erubescent, and which in the Originall, are *Iashabu,* and *Ieboshu,* which have a musicall, and harmonious sound, and agnomination in them, let me note thus much, even in that, that the Holy Ghost in penning the Scriptures delights himself, not only with a propriety, but with a delicacy, and harmony, and melody of language; with height of Metaphors, and other figures, which may work greater impressions upon the Readers, and not with barbarous, or triviall, or market, or homely language.[2]

Against eloquence, one has only to associate it with tempters, braggarts, harlots, liars, seducers, tricksters, politicians, and advertising agents. Or you could dismiss a piece of writing or speech by calling it fluent or mellifluous. Eloquence is morally irresponsible, we are warned, rotten with vanity. When we flow with eloquence, we are not inspired by the Muses, though we may think we are: on the contrary, we are blithely corrupt, our word is not our bond but boundlessly self-regarding. Eloquence does not represent the real, it replaces it with its own voice, complacently narcissist. It is the charisma of speech, claiming to transcend the proprieties of law, custom, and reference: an inspired grace, a favor, like the gift of tongues. In print, it is "fine writing" (*fine* a curling of the reader's lip). In favor of eloquence, one has to argue that it is—or can be—a sign of life, abundance, nonchalance, and freedom, a quality of expressiveness not to be denied, a grace of behavior. It can also be defended—or at worst excused—as the result of frustration, as Geoffrey Hill—speaking of style as I would of eloquence—said of the prose of Thomas Nashe and Robert Burton:

> It is as if the effort "to translate wisdom into political action" which baffled humanists like Elyot and Starkey translates itself, in the prose of Nashe and Burton, into the praxis of an individual style. The energy has to go somewhere; since it cannot realize itself as a legislative act, it turns back into the authority and eccentricity of style itself.[3]

But the same energy can appease or deflect frustration by taking satisfaction in its own processes. The author of *Ulysses* and *Finnegans Wake* shows no sign of political frustration or of trying to make up for worldly disappointments: his eloquence is self-delighting. In that respect, eloquence is a mark of invention rather than of communication, an intrinsic achievement rather than a device for getting something done. David Bromwich has commented on Hill's *Mystery of the Charity of Charles Péguy:*

> Like no other poem of the age, *The Mystery of the Charity of Charles Péguy* sustains a partly public meditation with continuous personal intensity. Its motive may be described as an attempt to hold poetry and history in a single thought. Yet its eloquence is direct, chaste, and declarative, checked only by the thought that all eloquence terminates in action.[4]

Surely not "all." Martin Luther King's "Letter from a Birmingham Jail" is eloquent and directed toward action, to shame "the white moderates" and the Christian Church in the South into coming forth for a just cause. But eloquence does not serve a purpose or an end in action. If Bromwich's last generalization were true, it would be necessary to regard eloquence as always ancillary to rhetoric, merely a means to another end. In rhetoric, one is trying to persuade someone to do something: in eloquence, one is discovering with delight the expressive resources of the means at hand. Eloquence is a promise of another kind of happiness, not an acquisition in the world but a token of other ways of being alive, in passing. It does this when it discloses a pitch of language—and therefore a flair of feeling and perception—in addition to, or even instead of, its standard referential duty. If, as Tzvetan Todorov says in his commentary on Bakhtin, "culture consists in the discourses retained by collective memory (the commonplaces and stereotypes just as much as the exceptional words), discourses in relation to which every uttering subject must situate himself or herself," the exceptional words are the constituents of eloquence, the flair of being alive.[5] The form of this flair need not be verbal. Eloquence is memorable speech, but there is eloquence in a phrase in music, a line in a painting, a curve in a work of architecture or sculpture, a shot in golf or tennis. There is eloquence even in a gesture of defeat, as Tony in *Scarface* sinks his face into a heap of cocaine on his desk before going through the inevitable motions of despair and mayhem. "Action is eloquence," as Volumnia tells her son Coriolanus, "and the eyes of th' ignorant / More learned than the ears" (3.2.76–77). The instances of eloquence that I remember, in the sense that they have lodged in my mind without effort on my part, are gratuitous, they stand alone as particles of language disclosed, inventions, things added to a life otherwise thought to be already known. I don't recall the context—or contexts, since it turns up more than once—of Pound's "In the gloom, the gold gathers the light against it." No matter;

it is probably a breath taken in freedom against the obligation of saying grim things. "I could not pick the arrows from my side" is from Hart Crane's *The Bridge*, but it floats nearly free in my mind. "I was the shadow of the waxwing slain / By the false azure in the windowpane" starts the poem in *Pale Fire*, but I recall nothing further of its setting. I agree that some eloquences stay in their settings, like the word *prevalent* in canto 28, where Pound tells of Clara Leonora

> and il Gran Maestro
> Mr Liszt had come to the home of her parents
> And taken her on his prevalent knee . . .[6]

Or like the Duke's saying to Claudio in *Measure for Measure:*

> Thou hast nor youth nor age,
> But, as it were, an after-dinner's sleep,
> Dreaming on both
> *(3.1.32–34)*

—though Eliot quoted those lines without context or ado as epigraph to "Gerontion." The first line of Hill's "Pavana Dolorosa"—"Loves I allow and passions I approve"—is eloquent by itself, but richer still in relation to the epigraph it recovers from Robert Southwell's "Marie Magdalens Funeral Teares":

> Passions I allow, and loves I approve, onely I would wishe that men would alter their object and better their intent.

But even if we think we know what we can say for eloquence, what does it say for itself; what is it for or against? It is against dullness, dryness, routine, habit, "the malady of the quotitian," the oppressiveness of one-damn-thing-after-another. It flourishes in a language and wants to have more abundant life there.

III

In chapter 17 of "The Window," the first part of *To the Light-house*, Mrs. Ramsay takes her place, tired and anxious, at the head of the dining table. Her husband is at the other end, and between them are the children—Rose, Roger, Andrew, Prue, Jasper—and the guests, William Bankes, Lily Briscoe, Paul Rayley, Minta Doyle, Charles Tansley, and Augustus Car-michael. The talk among the men is of politics, the crimes of the government. Meanwhile Mrs. Ramsay thinks of her life, what she has done with it and why it has come to so little, the intended trip to the lighthouse, her husband's character, the impressive parts of it and the harsh parts. Thirty pages later, the meal is nearly over when she hears Mr. Ramsay repeating something:

> and she knew it was poetry from the rhythm and the ring of exultation, and melancholy in his voice:
>
> > Come out and climb the garden gate,
> > > Luriana Lurilee.
> > The China rose is all abloom and buzzing
> > > with the
> > > Yellow bee.
>
> The words (she was looking at the window) sounded as if they were floating like flowers on water out there, cut off from them all, as if no one had said them, but they had come into existence of them-selves.
>
> "And all the lives we ever lived and all the lives to be are full of trees and changing leaves." She did not know what they meant, but, like music, the words seemed to be spoken by her own voice, outside her self, saying quite easily and naturally what had been

in her mind the whole evening while she said different things. She knew, without looking round, that every one at the table was listening to the voice saying:

I wonder if it seems to you,

Luriana, Lurilee

with the same sort of relief and pleasure that she had, as if this were, at last, the natural thing to say, this were their own voice speaking.[7]

It is the quality of eloquence in this passage that the words spoken by Mr. Ramsay, his intoning of stanzas from a poem by Charles Elton (1839-1900), seem—to Mrs. Ramsay—to enter the voices of everyone at the table and to speak what each of them wants to say, as distinct from the things they say on their own behalf. The meaning of "Luriana, Lurilee" is not an issue, it would make little difference if the poem were declared meaningless, "like music." In such a poem of incantation, syllable calls to syllable, word to word, exempt from duty or obligation. For as long as the recitation lasts, an official culture given to power and authority goes on vacation, hands itself over to the gratuitous authority of freedom, play, and pleasure. Eloquence is one of the forms of this gratuity. The most sensuous temptation it offers is that of staying on vacation forever, never leaving its precincts. Many writers have denounced eloquence for that reason. Fie on the eloquence that leaves us craving itself, not things: "Fi de l'éloquence qui nous laisse envie de soi, non des choses," Montaigne said in his "Consideration of Cicero."[8] John Locke took the same hard attitude, as we'll see. And Samuel Johnson in his preface to *A Dictionary of the English Language:* "I am not yet so lost in lexicography, as to forget that *words are the daughters of earth, and that things are the sons of heaven.*"[9]

Things, matter, content: these are the official constituents of meaning. Meaning—such as it is—is the protest an official culture makes against eloquence, against the freedoms it takes.[10] The eloquence of art arises from the misgiving a decent culture feels, from time to time, about the project of enforcing its category, that of being completely and insistently itself. Not that eloquence is the only unofficial form of being. Any experience that makes for chaos would serve just as well—Warren Smith's insanity in *Mrs. Dalloway,* for instance. The only necessary thing is to break the circuit of social mastery, if only for an interval.

Eloquence is a value, but a questionable and often a justly questioned one. Not everyone is thrilled—or ought to be—by the sounds of it. Even when we have been won over by its verve, we are not certain that we should have been; we may have been seduced by a charlatan or a presidential speechwriter. A particular occasion of eloquence may have no relation to wisdom, its traditional associate. The three classical motives of speech—to teach, to delight, to persuade, *docere, delectare, flectere*—are not necessarily of equal validity. In the fourth book of *De Doctrina Christiana,* Augustine acknowledged the necessity and the value of *delectare* but only in the service of something better, the crucial *docere.* The first consideration is to preach and teach the truth: it is never permissible to tell a lie, even in an ostensibly good cause. I remember from my school catechism: "No motive can excuse a lie, because a lie is always sinful and bad in itself." The best plan may be to think of eloquence as a neutral term, but then we have to decide whether or not it can be maintained in that state: maybe an instance of it should be pushed into a "good" or a "bad" bin. If good, we call it expressive; if bad, we call it sonorous or, far worse, charming. When a speaker or a writer favors a cause we admire and gives better reasons than we could have given in support of it, we say that the eloquence of the address is convincing, persuasive, or decisive. If we think the cause insidious or otherwise deplorable, we find the eloquence that served it cheap, specious, empty, sophistical, glib, or, more succinctly, damned lies. Edmund Burke showed his friend Philip Francis a draft of the *Reflections on the Revolution in France* that included a description of Marie Antoinette—"I saw her just above the horizon, decorating and cheering the elevated sphere she just began to move in,—glittering like the morning-star, full of life, and splendour, and joy. Oh! what a revolution! and what a heart must I have to contemplate without emotion that elevation and that fall!" Francis told Burke that the description was "pure foppery." [11] The passage—soon to be admired or denounced as one of the most eloquent pieces of writing in the English language—could not persuade Francis, steeled as his mind was against the queen. It made no difference to him that Burke presented her as a tragic heroine, to be pitied rather than judged; the pathos of the aesthetic image did not remove the animus that Francis had already settled for. Pathos is one of the resources of eloquence, but some people on some occasions are immune to it. The death of little Nell has driven many readers to tears, but some to tears of laughter. Eloquence resembles hang-gliding in some respects. It is an activity between sky and earth that, if done at all, should be done well. Done well, it is enjoyed by glider and spectator as a sign of freedom, if only relative freedom among the conditions that limit its range and duration. Life is a little richer because of it. The difference between eloquence and hang-gliding is that when hang-gliding fails, the glider is killed; when eloquence fails, the result is merely embarrassment, a temporary instance of shame.

But then there are adjudications in the middle of the case: we say that a speech or an essay is "elegant," but we haven't declared our hand, we haven't indicated whether we regard elegance as a good or a bad quality, a vice of style the property of cads or one of its higher virtues. Remarking that someone's style is sociable, we probably mean that on the whole it's a worthy thing, or at worst better than its sullen opposite. But if we say, with Kenneth Burke, that "in its simplest manifestation, style is ingratiation," specifically "an attempt to gain favour by the hypnotic or suggestive process of 'saying the right thing,'" we may rest in the pleasure of being gratified, or find it disgusting that anyone should take such stock in gaining our favor.[12] The same difficulty holds with other values. Truth is good, but it is not always decent to tell it, spilling it out when it is likely to hurt someone's feelings. Courage is a virtue, when we think of it as brave or fearless, but it becomes a doubtful attribute when we call it intrepid, and a vice when we call someone's actions audacious or foolhardy. Intelligence is a value, but not when we call an exemplar of it brilliant or clever—which are no longer terms of praise but more-or-less bitter recognitions of a capacity we assure ourselves we wouldn't want to have even if we could. So with eloquence. We like to think of ourselves as articulate, but not fast-talking or glib. It is a relief to be able to say what we want to say, but we think the gift of the gab a poor endowment, and we are content to assign it to car salesmen, stand-up comedians, and Irishmen.

Eloquence is speech in excess of expectation, a coloratura flourish; it arises when modesty has been set aside and decorum put in question. It is at least remotely derived from the violence of the gods; first physical violence, then violence extended to words as magic. The curse is magical through the mere fact of its being uttered. Speech is to be feared, hence the prestige of euphemism, silence, and the act of quietly naming something.[13] The Sublime is the mode in which this divine violence is recognized, all the more vigorously when it appears to be incited by the natural world—mountain gloom and mountain glory. But there is a strong tradition in which such violence is feared and rebuked. I have quoted from Paul's second letter to the Corinthians, where he speaks of a man "caught up into paradise" who "heard unspeakable words, which it is not lawful for a man to utter" (2 Cor. 12:4). Presumably it is not lawful because such a man would be aspiring to transcend the categorical limits of his being human, trying to become angelic. He speaks in tongues, deliberately one supposes, and commits the sin of pride in an outrageous form. So Paul in both epistles to the Corinthians keeps saying that his own form of preaching is the honorable one—"And my speech and my preaching was not with enticing words of man's wisdom, but in demonstration of the Spirit and of power" (1 Cor. 2:4)—and straightforward—"Seeing then that we have such hope, we use great plainness of speech" (2 Cor. 3:12). He also tells his flock in Corinth to give up their dissentions and all "speak the same thing" (1 Cor. 1:10). Evidently he has in view the sophistic practices of orators and their contaminating effect on the Corinthians.[14] But it is not graceful, even in Paul, to draw attention to your style and claim that it's the proper one. A Corinthian might say: "I'll be the judge of that, if you don't mind." Besides, it is permissible to enjoy a burst of eloquence for its own sake. Even Polonius did, when he heard the First Player. Hamlet wondered about "the mobled queen," but Polonius interjected: "That's good; 'mobled queen' is good" (2.2).

The safest attitude—if we want to be safe—is the middle-of-the-road prudence that Robert Graves recommends in "The Cool Web":

> Children are dumb to say how hot the day is,
> How hot the scent is of the summer rose . . .

"Dumb," not in the American sense of "stupid," but in the standard English sense of speechless or inexpressive. Western cultures think it important that we express ourselves and—better still, and more difficult—say how other things are; though I have never heard it insisted on that we should be able to say precisely how hot the day is, how hot—why hot?—the scent is of the summer rose, or measure the relative dreadfulnesses of "the black wastes of evening sky" and "the tall soldiers drumming by." But, the poem says, "we"—meaning adults—"have speech, to chill the angry day" and "to dull the rose's cruel scent." Why the day is thought to be angry and yet susceptible to being chilled, and the scent cruel yet mitigable by being dulled, and how speech can effect these alleviations, the poem does not say. "There's a cool web of language winds us in," that keeps us from flying off into extremes of joy or fear. In the end, it evidently won't make much difference:

> We grow sea-green at last and coldly die
> In brininess and volubility.

The deep blue sea will get us, and we'll die screaming, salt in our lungs, talkative to the end:

> But if we let our tongues lose self-possession,
> Throwing off language and its watery clasp
> Before our death, instead of when death comes,
> Facing the wide glare of the children's day,
> Facing the rose, the dark sky and the drums,
> We shall go mad no doubt and die that way.[15]

The poem is a defense of the kind of poetry that Graves wrote: observing the "genius" of standard English, and silently rebuking those poets—Eliot and Pound, I think he had in mind—who were enchanted by bizarre idiolects, mostly French and Italian. Graves seems to claim that these poets gave up the sane resources of English, the middle or civic style, and fell for the glamour of foreign eloquence. That way, madness and America lie.

But Graves hasn't given up his own claim to eloquence:

> We spell away the overhanging night,
> We spell away the soldiers and the fright.[16]

Children grow up by learning to spell, gaining access to feasible forms of magic and wisdom, moving among the native myths, forms of eloquence they have not invented. The most effective teaching method is repetition, the creative force of rote. "We spell away . . . We spell away . . ." "We spell away the soldiers and the fright" is notably eloquent, far-rangingly memorable, an instance of the verbal magic it invokes.

Prudence is, I suppose, a virtue, but not an exciting or invigorating one. In "Open House" Theodore Roethke claims to speak without the constraints of language: "I have no need for tongue," he says, tonguing his way from claim to claim. "My heart keeps open house." If he is only angry enough, his anger will speak directly for him, getting rid of linguistic disguise. But even though he is naked, he is not naked enough, nakedness is his shield. "Myself is what I wear," he writes, not asking what is under the clothes. The poem expresses the desire—which Roethke often presents as already accomplished—to circumvent language and let "my truths" utter themselves without the forgone impediments of syntax. "The deed will speak the truth / In language strict and pure." Hence the truth-telling power of anger, rage, agony: these emotions "stop the lying mouth."[17] Why the mouth lies, the poem does not say. Original Sin, presumably. Eliot wrote of simplicity as an achievement won despite the sin of language:

> Great simplicity is only won by an intense moment
> or by years of intelligent effort, or by both. It rep-

resents one of the most arduous conquests of the
human spirit: the triumph of feeling and thought
over the natural sin of language.[18]

This is not as clear as it appears. Christopher Ricks has interpreted the sin as "something that is distinguishable from but
not distinct from the original sin that infects even language,"
but how it can be distinguished from that, he has not said; or
how a language can be said to be in a state of sin.[19] If there is
natural sin, it is not clear who the sinner is, though I suspect
that anyone who tries to be eloquent is in danger of specific or
actual sin.

But it is vulgar to ask someone to speak well and then impose
on him or her the additional duty of appearing to speak well by
nature rather than by art. In the most eloquent passages, so far
as I recall them, the expression seems to surprise itself, being
more than adequate to the occasion, such that we don't feel
impelled to ask whether the writer is showing off or not.

IV

The standard argument against eloquence is that it is morally
indifferent, it shows one's determination to speak vividly,
whether what one is saying is true or false. To acquire immunity to eloquence is therefore, as Bertrand Russell said, of the
utmost importance to the citizens of a democracy. It is just as
important, as I don't recall Russell saying, to the citizens of a
dictatorship, who find immunity harder to acquire. In a democracy, you can usually stay away from the big talk. The force of
eloquence at the Nuremberg rallies was not in anything Hitler,
Goebbels, or Rosenberg said but in the press of the crowd, the
people gathered in the powerless power of unison. Their eloquence did not need words, the throng was expressive in itself,

whatever it "said." Ancient rhetoric taught students—and some modern debating societies still do—how to argue disinterestedly on either side of a question. Lawyers, journalists, and politicians are trained in this tradition, keeping a straight face the while. They can, with equal force, defend a vice or the specious appearance of a virtue. As Donne wrote in the "Litanie":

> When we are moved to seem religious
> Only to vent wit, Lord deliver us.[20]

"Are moved," as if we thought ourselves more sinned against than sinning.

I'll refer to four versions (among many) of the common case against eloquence: they are by a poet, Donne, the philosophers Locke and Husserl, and the critic Hugh Kenner. Their approaches are different, even if the case is the same.

Donne's arises in one of his *Paradoxes and Problems*, or rather in the problem in which he asks "Why Venus starre onely doth cast a Shadowe?" Problems of this kind were devised for university teaching, questions-and-answers to sharpen a student's skill in dialectic. They were also featured at dinner parties and other social occasions to display one's verbal dexterity.[21] Donne treats them as conceits, so it is hard to know where he stands with them between jest and earnest. He wrote the Problems in his declining years, to amuse himself. Whether Venus or Mercury is nearer the earth depends, I gather, on whether you accept the astronomy of Ptolemy or of Copernicus and Tycho Brahe. In the present problem Donne took the Ptolemaic position that Mercury was nearer, but in the "Second Anniversary" he held to the Copernican conclusion that Venus is nearer. It hardly matters, because after the first sentence in the problem he gives up talking astronomy and changes over to Venus as goddess of love and Mercury as god of eloquence. He's really talking about sex, marriage, and other forms of seduction; his professed fear of eloquence—the eloquence of others, not one's own—is that it works its will on you unawares:

> Is it because the workes of *Venus* neede shadowing covering and disguising? But those of *Mercury* neede it more. For Eloquence, his occupation, is all shadowes and colours. Let our life bee a sea, and then our reason, and even passions, are wind enough to carry us whither wee should goe, but Eloquence is a storme and tempest that miscarries us. And who doubts that Eloquence (which must perswade people to take a yoake of Soveraignty and then beg and make lawes to tye them faster, and then give monny to the Invention, repayr and strengthen it) needs more shadowes and colourings then to perswade any man or woman to that which is naturall, And *Venus* markets are so naturall, that when wee sollicite the best way (which is by marriage) our perswasions worke not so much to drawe a woman to us, as against her nature, to drawe her from all others besides, And so when wee goe against nature and from *Venus* workes (for Marriage is chastity) wee neede shadowes and colours, but not else. . . . So then *Venus* flyes not light so much as *Mercury*, who creeping into our understanding in our darkenesse, were defeated if hee were perceived. Then eyther this Shadowe confesseth that same darke Melancholly repentence which accompanies it. Or that so violent fires neede some shadowy refreshing and intermission, Or else Light signifying both day and youth, and shadowe both Night and Age, Shee pronounceth, by this, that shee professeth both all times and persons.[22]

Eloquence, then, works best in darkness, when we can't see anything and can't fend off the seductive words which "creep into our understanding," like the serpent tempting Eve. "Our ears, eyes of the darkness," as Joyce calls them in *Finnegans Wake*, are open, day and night, to the acoustic disturbances around us.[23] "Were defeated if hee were perceived": again like the serpent, who was not perceived for what he was till it was too late. So men are deceived by the lore of sex, love, and marriage to the extent of taking up their yoke of sovereignty, binding themselves to it, and paying good money to keep it going. As if this institution were not enough, men are also deceived by the wiles of words. The admonition comes from Dr. Donne, notoriously wily in his words.

Locke is a more stolid writer than Donne, more systematic in his attack on the cheating capacity of words—especially in philosophic discourse—and more dogged in listing their imperfections, as in the chapter headings of book 3, chapter 10—"Of the Abuse of Words"—of *An Essay Concerning Human Understanding:*

> *First*, "Words without any or without clear ideas,"
> *Secondly*, "Unsteady application of them," *Thirdly*,
> "affected obscurity by wrong application," *Fourthly*,
> "Taking them for things," *Fifthly*, "setting them for
> what they cannot signify," *Sixthly*, "A supposition
> that words have a certain and evident signification,"
> and *Seventhly*, "Figurative speech also an abuse of
> language."

This last is the most vehement part of the attack, where Locke denounces the eloquence of figurative language but resorts to the most blatant rhetorical figure in doing so. The gist of his attack is that figurative language must be tolerated in "harangues and popular addresses," but not in serious speech and writing:

Since wit and fancy finds easier entertainment in the world than dry truth and real knowledge, *figurative speeches* and allusion in language will hardly be admitted as *an* imperfection or *abuse* of it. I confess, in discourses where we seek rather pleasure and delight than information and improvement, such ornaments as are borrowed from them can scarce pass for faults. But yet, if we would speak of things as they are, we must allow that all the art of rhetoric, besides order and clearness, all the artificial and figurative application of words eloquence hath invented, are for nothing else but to insinuate wrong *ideas,* move the passions, and thereby mislead the judgment, and so indeed are perfect cheat; and therefore however laudable or allowable oratory may render them in harangues and popular addresses, they are certainly, in all discourses that pretend to inform or instruct, wholly to be avoided and, where truth and knowledge are concerned, cannot but be thought a great fault either of the language or person that makes use of them. What and how various they are will be superfluous here to take notice, the books of rhetoric which abound in the world will instruct those who want to be informed; only I cannot but observe how little the preservation and improvement of truth and knowledge is the care and concern of mankind, since the arts of fallacy are endowed and preferred. It is evident how much men love to deceive and be deceived, since rhetoric, that powerful instrument of error and deceit, has its established professors, is publicly taught, and has always been had in great reputation; and I doubt not but it will be thought great boldness, if not brutality, in me to have said thus much against it. *Eloquence,* like the fair sex, has too prevailing beauties in it to suffer itself ever to be spoken against. And it is in vain to find fault with those arts of deceiving wherein men find pleasure to be deceived.[24]

A joke, maybe, but the talk is again of sex, inevitably once Locke has adverted to "how much men love to deceive and be deceived." The arts of fallacy may be active in philosophy, but deceiving and being deceived are chiefly rampant in social and sexual life. "It will be thought great boldness, if not brutality, in me to have said thus much against it": the *it* can only be the institution of women as objects of desire. "*Eloquence,* like the fair sex" starts a sentence that has to allude to "beauties," just as the whole paragraph reaches back to "ornaments" and culminates in "pleasure to be deceived." Locke's position on women and their subjection to their husbands was inconsistent. Against Robert Filmer, he maintained that the apparent secondariness of Eve to Adam was no argument for the constitutional inequality of women to men.[25] He had a quarrel with language; he thought that our linguistic habits were infatuated by the external appearances of things rather than attentive to their true, interior qualities. In speech, he argued, differences in nature were regularly set aside in favor of conventional linguistic categories. When he referred to Eloquence, in the passage I've quoted, he personified it clearly enough as an upper-class woman, rotten with affectation and sensuality, sought out by aristocratic gentlemen; a scandal by comparison with the honest, hardworking men and women he professed to admire.

The passages differ most in their tones. Locke finds himself in the hopeless position of trying to keep himself free of figures while denouncing them. The connection between eloquence, beauty, the "flowers," and women was a long-established source of annoyance or amusement. Latin satire was the origin of it. Locke chooses to be exacerbated. Glancing aside for a moment: Sidney, in the *Defence of Poesie*, where his theme is the vanity of poetic diction, is ruefully urbane:

> Now, for the out-side of it, which is words, or (as I may tearme it) Diction, it is even well worse. So is that hony-flowing Matron *Eloquence* appareled, or rather disguised, in a Curtisan-like painted affectation: one time with so farre fetched words, that many seeme Monsters, but must seeme strangers to any poore English man; another tyme, with coursing of a letter, as if they were bound to followe the method of a Dictionary; an other tyme, with figures and flowers, extremely winter-starved.[26]

Donne isn't troubled by the large quandaries of language, so he plays freely among the local counters of seeing and hearing, shadows and colors. Eloquence to Donne and Locke is a failing, a consequence of Original Sin, a *culpa, felix* or not, at best an unfortunate necessity, like women to men. You can either resent the way life is ordained, or be intrigued by it. As in Marvell's "The Garden": "Two Paradises / 'twere in one / To live in Paradise alone." Neither Donne nor Locke had the privilege of reading Beckett's *Malone Dies*, in which we are instructed that "there is no use indicting words, they are no shoddier than what they peddle."[27] Or his "The End": "Even the words desert you, it's as bad as that."[28]

Husserl's opposition to eloquence, especially in "The Origin of Geometry," arises from his care that a proper language be available to science and logic. "Proper" is what he calls "univocal." An improper language is one that feeds passively on association, cultural sedimentation, and equivocity:

It is easy to see that even in [ordinary] human life, and first of all in every individual life from childhood up to maturity, the originally intuitive life which creates its originally self-evident structures through activities on the basis of sense-experience very quickly and in increasing measure falls victim to the *seduction of language*. Greater and greater segments of this life lapse into a kind of talking and reading that is dominated purely by association; and often enough, in respect to the validities arrived at in this way, it is disappointed by subsequent experience.

Husserl's response to this habit of language is "to put a stop to the free play of associative constructions." They are "a constant danger." To thwart them, scientists must be vigilant and hold to "the univocity of linguistic expression and to securing, by means of the most painstaking formation of the relevant words, propositions, and complexes of propositions, the results which are to be univocally expressed." They must "maintain the constant claim, the personal certainty, that everything they put into scientific assertions has been said 'once and for all,' that it 'stands fast,' forever identically repeatable with self-evidence and usable for further theoretical or practical ends—as indubitably reactivatable with the identity of its actual meaning." It is not enough that scientists inherit the propositions of their disciplines and the logical methods of constructing new propositions: they must also learn, instructed by tradition, to "reactivate the primal beginnings," that is, "the sources of meaning for everything that comes later."[29]

It follows, as Derrida remarks in his commentary on "The Origin of Geometry," that "a poetic language, whose significations would not be *objects*, will never have any transcendental value for [Husserl]." Indeed, words and language in general "are not and can never be absolute *objects*." They do not possess "any resistant and permanent identity that is absolutely their own." They have their linguistic being "from an intention that traverses them as mediations." The "same" word is always "other," Derrida says, "according to the always different intentional acts which thereby make a word significative [*significant*]."[30] I assume that Husserl's attitude toward eloquence can safely be inferred from his revulsion against profundity, sedimentation, and equivocation:

> Profundity [*Tiefsinn*] is a mark of the chaos that genuine science wants to transform into a cosmos, into a simple, completely clear, lucid order. Genuine science, so far as its real doctrine extends, knows no profundity.[31]

Derrida remarks:

> Because it brings everything to view within a present act of evidence, because nothing is hidden or announced in the penumbra of potential intentions, because it has mastered all the dynamics of sense, univocal language remains *the same*. It thus keeps its ideal identity throughout all cultural development.

It is also endlessly transparent, translatable. Noting that equivocity is the mark of every culture, Derrida opposes to Husserl's univocity Joyce's equivocation, presumably in the later chapters of *Ulysses* and in *Finnegans Wake,* his decision "to repeat and take responsibility for all equivocation itself, utilizing a language that could equalize the greatest possible synchrony with the greatest potential for buried, accumulated, and interwoven intentions within each linguistic atom, each vocable, each word, each simple proposition, in all wordly cultures and their most ingenious forms (mythology, religion, sciences, arts, literature, politics, philosophy, and so forth)." Joyce cultivates the associative syntheses rather than avoiding them, and "rediscovers the poetic value of passivity."[32]

It may be asked: perhaps Husserl's insistence on univocity applies only to his concern for science and scientists, and like Locke he was more relaxed about informal speech and conversation? His references to the seductive power of language and our tendency to be seduced by it do not suggest that he smiled on equivocation, sedimentation, and excess in the home or the street. I know of no evidence that he took pleasure in vivacities of language.

Hugh Kenner's asperity toward eloquence—which he regularly called sonority—arose from two considerations. One: the relation, in Elizabethan song, between words and music, such that the words hardly mattered and might not even be sufficiently heard to be understood. They were in the song only to carry the voice. Much the same applies to opera in a foreign language. Those who go to the Metropolitan Opera to hear an opera in Italian, German, or French may not understand a word of it, and may depend for help on supertitles, but they are thrilled by the sounds, especially by tenor and soprano, and take the details of the plot from the little the program notes tell of it. Two: in the Elizabethan theater, the words assigned to actors often forced the audience to dream away from the visible. When Marlowe wrote of Helen of Troy, "Was this the face that launched a thousand ships / And burned the topless towers of Ilium?" what the audience saw was merely a painted boy strutting across the stage.

Kenner's allegiance was to things seen by an alert mind, the project of Objectivism in modern poetry by which language directs the mind from one intelligible object of attention to the next, never allowing it to sink to rest upon a succulent cadence. He admired Pound more than any other modern poet for that reason, and elucidated his poetic values—Pound, who urged modern poets to cultivate the virtues of good prose, especially good nineteenth-century French prose, as in Stendhal and Flaubert. In his early years Pound approved of Ford Madox Ford's style rather than Yeats's because Yeats was susceptible to the glamour of the associations that hung near words, whereas Ford was willing to use any words that enacted the application of intelligence to the matter in hand. Kenner, like Pound, regarded eloquence not as a value to be sought for its own sake but as a quality that might—or might not—attend the mind in its movement among the constituents of the world. His attitude to Eliot and to Yeats was therefore ambiguous; he wrote well about them, but he could not approve their susceptibility to the velleities of Symbolism.

V

The best argument for eloquence is that it is a skill and therefore an imperative. If you think you're good at something, you do it, even at the cost of wasting your life in its service. A writer who, on a particular day of need, can't find the words is appalled and terrified that he'll never find them again. In Donne's "Epithalamion at the Marriage of the Earl of Somerset," one of the speakers, Idios, making excuses for his absence from the court and his decision to go into the country for a while, receives a rebuke from Allophanes and answers:

> I knew
> All this, and onely therefore I withdrew.
> To know and feele all this, and not to have
> Words to express it, makes a man a grave

Of his owne thoughts; I would not therefore stay
At a great feast, having no Grace to say.[33]

If the question of egotism is raised, you can answer that the words you want to find for yourself are in the language anyhow, even if they're hiding, so it's only decent to bring their beauties out: it's like doing the best you can for your country. Like hang-gliding again: practicing a skill, you feel like a bird, wings outspread, capitalizing on the constraints that commonly weigh you down. The constraints—or the sins—are in language, so you exercise your talent for finding ways of circumventing them, ways of being free, or enjoying the exhilaration of feeling free. Besides, eloquence may serve a good cause, as in the *Eumenides*. Persuasion watched over Athena while she urged the Erinyes to find Orestes innocent and to commit themselves to Athens in peace. In such a case you have the double best of the situation. But you must start by taking pleasure in the means, not merely in the end. Even if you lose the case, you should feel satisfaction in the skill with which you advocated it: lost causes are not always a dead loss. Kenneth Burke again, on the "categorical appeal" of literature:

> Eloquence, by stressing the means of literature, requires an interest in the means as ends. Otherwise eloquence becomes an obstacle to enjoyment. Readers who seek in art a substitute for living will find the Stendhal procedure [—Each sentence in Stendhal deliberately eschews any saliency as a minor or incidental form—it aims to be imperceptible—and if the reader forgets that he is reading, he is reading as Stendhal would have him read—] most acceptable; a novelist like the Hugo of *L'Homme qui rit* will annoy them with his bristling epigrammatic

"unreality," a kind of saliency so thoroughly literary that, however strong the readers' impressions, they can never forget that the book was "written." The primary purpose of eloquence is not to enable us to live our lives on paper—it is to convert life into its most thorough verbal equivalent. The categorical appeal of literature resides in a liking for verbalization as such, just as the categorical appeal of music resides in a liking for musical sounds as such. The stressing of a medium requires a preference for this medium—and thus in eloquence, which is the maximum stressing of the literary medium, we may find evidence of a "categorical appeal."[34]

We can stretch this a little by saying that one of the aims of speech and writing is the conversion of the shapelessness of a life into the formal felicity of eloquence, and we are likely to be especially gratified by those occasions in which we find ourselves paying just as much attention to the way in which something is said as to the said thing. Or just as much attention to the trajectory of a sentence as to the outcome of it, the completed meaning. The meaning is over, but you have had the pleasure of seeing it rise, shine, and fall. Sometimes this pleasure is rejected; as Greta Scacchi says to Tim Robbins in *The Player:* "Words, I like words. I'm not crazy about complete sentences." But this is unusual. In Donne's "The Exstasie" the pleasure we take in the eloquence of these two stanzas strikes us a few seconds before we can be sure—if we ever can—what the speaker is saying:

> As our blood labours to beget
>   Spirits, as like soules as it can,
> Because such fingers need to knit
>   That subtile knot, which makes us man:

> So must pure lovers soules descend
>   T'affections, and to faculties,
> Which sense may reach and apprehend,
>   Else a great Prince in prison lies.[35]

The force of eloquence in the last line is irresistible, partly because of the strong internal alliteration of *Prince* and *prison*, partly because of the monosyllabic *lies* completing the rhyme of *faculties*. But the line in its context is not perspicuous. One of the capacities of eloquence is to try to make us ignore the context and remember only the eloquent words as if they floated free of it. Is the last line as erotic as it seems, the Prince the phallus that shouldn't be idle? Paul Muldoon evidently thinks so, in his recent poem "Sillyhow Stride" —

> every full-length cross-carrier almost certainly up to
>   some sort of high jinks
> else a great Prince in prison lies.[36]

Or is the Prince, as Helen Gardner maintains, the soul? The soul should "perform its divinely appointed function" of governing the activities of the body. If it doesn't, it is like a prince in prison. "The concordance of Donne's poems shows how fond he is of the metaphor of the soul as prince and the body, with its limbs, as his province." If the soul doesn't "animate the body in all its parts, it is imprisoned in a carcass instead of reigning in its kingdom."[37] Donne liked the soul-and-prison motif well enough to advert to it in his letters, as in this one to Sir Henry Goodyer:

> Our nature is Meteorique, we respect (because we
> partake so) both earth and heaven; for as our bodies
> glorified shall be capable of spirituall joy, so our souls
> demerged into those bodies, are allowed to partake
> earthly pleasure. Our soul is not sent hither, only

to go back again: we have some errand to do here:
nor is it sent into prison, because it comes innocent:
and he which sent it, is just.[38]

The opposing interpretation to Gardner's maintains that with
the word *descend* the poem puts an end to its spiritual "ecstasy"
and turns to the body. Gardner wants to keep the poem Platonic to the end. "The only plea made in these lines (ll. 49–76) is
that the lovers' souls should return from their ecstatic commu-
nion to reanimate their bodies."[39] William Empson thinks the
Platonic emphasis would make the poem insipid: "An eruption
of passion was to be expected after the long spiritual ecstasy, as
was so often found at revivalist camp meetings."[40] A strange
feature of the last line, as of many other eloquent passages, is
how blithely it seems to accommodate rival meanings. If we
find it unforgettable, we easily carry the embarrassment of not
having decided what it purports.

VI

This makes a problem for eloquence; we like it too much, it offers
itself to all our seasons. In this it is like the trope in Stevens's
poem "The Motive for Metaphor," according to which we like
metaphor in autumn when "everything is half dead" and again
in spring when, "desiring the exhilarations of changes," we
are content with "things that would never be quite expressed"
and we are never quite ourselves or feel the need to be. What
we shrink from is "the weight of primary noon,/The ABC of
being," in the end "the vital, arrogant, fatal, dominant X."[41] I
take the X to be the insistence of meaning, or of anything that
too harshly asserts itself, beyond change. Eloquence, like metaphor, offers itself nonchalantly and is indifferent to contexts and
formulations.

And even to communication, if by that word we have social amenity in mind. Adorno said, in a characteristically severe
essay:

> That works renounce communication is a neces-
> sary yet by no means sufficient condition of their
> unideological essence. The central criterion is the
> force of expression, through the tension of which
> artworks become eloquent with wordless gesture.
> In expression they reveal themselves as the wounds
> of society; expression is the social ferment of their
> autonomous form.[42]

Explaining *wounds* and the dissonant, contradictory quality
of the art that Adorno favors, his translator Robert Hullot-
Kentor remarks that "eloquence" is not a satisfactory translation
of Adorno's "Sprachcharakter." The English concept "tends to
emphasize an unconflicted sort of fluency and persuasiveness":

> Adorno, however, is not at all concerned with per-
> suasion but rather with expression as gesture, cipher,
> countenance, script and speech as it arises out of
> brokenness, fragmentariness or fissuredness.[43]

It seems to be another version of Adorno's admonition: no
poems after Auschwitz. Or at any rate, no poems forgetful of
Auschwitz. No eloquence without a sense of the feelings that
have not survived, deleted by those that have.

Adorno's stricture is too hard to be borne. Nor has it silenced
poets or novelists. Life must (if possible) go on. Perhaps the
only tribute one can pay to Adorno is to remember him and retain a scruple in favor of his testament, even while one goes on.
A scruple is as much as can be sustained. A further possibility is
to give up magniloquence and let eloquence inhabit the entire
work, the form of it, rather than break out into local incandes-

cences of style. A version of this eloquence of form might be the wit that Eliot admired in Marvell's poetry, "a tough reasonableness beneath the slight lyric grace."[44]

VII

In chapter 19 of "The Window," Mrs. Ramsay goes into the library—or into the room that passes for a library—and takes up her knitting. Her husband is already there, reading Scott's *The Antiquary*, the chapter of Steenie's drowning and Mucklebackit's sorrow. He reads it with sympathy almost to tears. Then he backs away to appreciate the quality of the book. "Well, let them improve upon that, he thought as he finished the chapter." And this sets him thinking about literature in general, what's good and what's not, the young men who care for this sort of thing and those who don't. Meanwhile Mrs. Ramsay has put aside her knitting and taken up a book—an anthology of Elizabethan poetry, apparently:

> And she opened the book and began reading here and there at random, and as she did so she felt that she was climbing backwards, upwards, shoving her way up under petals that curved over her, so that she only knew this is white, or this is red. She did not know at first what the words meant at all.
>
> > Steer, hither steer your winged pines, all beaten Mariners
>
> she read and turned the page, swinging herself, zigzagging this way and that, from one line to another as from one branch to another, from one red and white flower to another, until a little sound roused her—her husband slapping his thighs.[45]

Husband and wife continue reading, but in different ways. He projects himself imaginatively into the scene, she climbs branch by branch or rung by rung of Jacob's ladder to an aesthetic sense of the work. Each brings into the reading whatever he or she has retained from the evening, the conversations at dinner among the larger dissatisfactions. Mrs. Ramsay turns the pages and finds Shakespeare's sonnet 98:

> From you have I been absent in the spring,
> When proud-pied April dress'd in all his trim
> Hath put a spirit of youth in every thing,
> That heavy Saturn laugh'd and leap'd with him.
> Yet nor the lays of birds nor the sweet smell
> Of different flowers in odour and in hue
> Could make me any summer's story tell,
> Or from their proud lap pluck them where they grew;
> Nor did I wonder at the lily's white,
> Nor praise the deep vermilion in the rose;
> They were but sweet, but figures of delight,
> Drawn after you, you pattern of all those.
>> Yet seem'd it winter still, and, you away,
>> As with your shadow I with these did play.[46]

[Mrs. Ramsay] was climbing up those branches, this way and that, laying hands on one flower and then another.

"Nor praise the deep vermilion in the rose," she read, and so reading she was ascending, she felt, on to the top, on to the summit. How satisfying! How restful! All the odds and ends of the day stuck to this magnet; her mind felt swept, felt clean. And then there it was, suddenly entire; she held it in her hands, beautiful and reasonable, clear and complete, the essence sucked out of life and held rounded here—the sonnet.[47]

Mrs. Ramsay is sensitive to the local flourish of eloquence, the line that breaks loose from its context as if, having its song, it had no need of meaning—"Nor praise the deep vermilion in the rose." We have a line of monosyllables, interrupted by the aria in three syllables—"vermilion"—complicating the music of the iambic pentameter but not disowning it:

> As with your shadow I with these did play,
> she murmured, putting the book on the table.[48]

Mrs. Ramsay's way of reciting the last line is in keeping with her sense of the work as a whole, "the sonnet," its eloquence of form incorporating without fuss the local beauty of the vermilion line. She does not trouble herself to interpret the poem—is it an excuse for the speaker's infidelities?—while she absorbs it into her otherwise anxious life. Not that the eloquence of the sonnet dissolves her anxiety: that would be too much to ask.

NOTES

CHAPTER I
Taking Notes

1. All biblical quotations are from the King James Version (Cambridge: Cambridge University Press, n.d.).

2. Julia Kristeva, "Word, Dialogue, and Novel," in *The Kristeva Reader*, ed. Toril Moi (New York: Columbia University Press, 1986), 54.

3. Friedrich Nietzsche, *Thus Spoke Zarathustra*, in *The Portable Nietzsche*, ed. and trans. Walter Kaufman (New York: Viking, 1954), 329. I am grateful to James Rolleston for suggesting modifications to the translation.

4. T. W. Adorno, *Minima Moralia: Reflections from Damaged Life*, trans. E. F. N. Jephcott (London: NLB, 1974), 222.

5. Geoffrey H. Hartman, *The Fateful Question of Culture* (New York: Columbia University Press, 1997), 18.

6. Richard Foster Jones, *The Triumph of the English Language: A Survey of Opinions Concerning the Vernacular from the Introduction of Printing to the Restoration* (Stanford: Stanford University Press, 1953), 168.

7. Quoted ibid., 115.

8. Nancy Struever, "Lorenzo Valla: Humanist Rhetoric and the Critique of the Classical Languages of Morality," in *Renaissance Eloquence: Studies in the Theory and Practice of Renaissance Rhetoric*, ed. James J. Murphy (Berkeley: University of California Press, 1983), 204.

9. Cf. Brian Vickers, "'The Power of Persuasion': Images of the Orator, Elyot to Shakespeare," in Murphy, *Renaissance Eloquence*, 412.

10. David Hume, "Of Eloquence," in *Essays Moral, Political and Literary* (London: Oxford University Press, 1966 rpt.), 103, 107, 109.

11. David Hume, "Of National Characters," *Essays*, 211.

12. Hume, "Of Eloquence," 104.

13. Samuel Johnson, Preface to *A Dictionary of the English Language* (1755), in *Johnson on the English Language*, ed. Gwin J. Kolb and Robert Demaria Jr. (New Haven: Yale University Press, 2005), 74, 79, 96–97, 108.

14. Ibid., 109.

15. William Wordsworth, Preface to the Second Edition of *Lyrical Ballads* (1800), in *Selected Poems and Prefaces,* ed. Jack Stillinger (Boston: Houghton Mifflin, 1965), 449.

16. Samuel Taylor Coleridge, *Biographia Literaria,* ed. James Engell and W. Jackson Bate (Princeton: Princeton University Press, 1983), 2: 143.

17. Geoffrey H. Hartman, *Minor Prophecies: The Literary Essay in the Culture Wars* (Cambridge: Harvard University Press, 1991), 11.

18. Cf. Donald C. Freeman, "'According to My Bond': *King Lear* and Re-cognition," in *The Stylistics Reader: From Roman Jakobson to the Present,* ed. Jean Jacques Weber (London: Arnold, 1996), 280–97.

19. Hartman, *Minor Prophecies,* 12.

20. Walt Whitman, "Out of the Cradle Endlessly Rocking," in *Complete Poetry and Collected Prose,* ed. Justin Kaplan (New York: Library of America, 1982), 393–94.

21. Edgar Allan Poe, "The Raven," in *Selected Writings,* ed. David Galloway (Baltimore: Penguin, 1967), 79. See Guy Davenport, *The Death of Picasso: New and Selected Writing* (Washington, D.C.: Shoemaker and Hoard, 2003), 87.

22. Angus Fletcher, *Colors of the Mind: Conjectures on Thinking in Literature* (Cambridge: Harvard University Press, 1991), 260.

23. Lionel Trilling, "On the Teaching of Modern Literature," in *Beyond Culture: Essays on Literature and Learning* (New York: Viking, 1965), 5–6.

24. On middlebrow culture see John Guillory, "The Ordeal of Middlebrow Culture," *Transition* 67 (1995): 87.

25. Michael Baxandall, *Giotto and the Orators: Humanist Observers of Painting in Italy and the Discovery of Pictorial Composition, 1350–1450* (Oxford: Clarendon, 1971), 45.

26. Quoted and translated by Charles S. Singleton, *An Essay on the "Vita Nuova"* (Cambridge: Harvard University Press, 1958), 85.

27. Quoted in Linda Dowling, *Language and Decadence in the Victorian Fin de Siècle* (Princeton: Princeton University Press, 1986), 133.

CHAPTER 2

The Latin Factor

1. James Joyce, *A Portrait of the Artist as a Young Man,* ed. Seamus Deane (New York: Penguin, 1992), 74–75.

2. James Joyce, *Ulysses,* ed. Hans Walter Gabler (New York: Random House, 1986), 353.

3. Cf. Walter J. Ong, "Wit and Mystery: A Revaluation in Mediaeval Latin Hymnody," *Speculum* 22, no. 3 (1947): 317–18.

4. Cf. Mary Carruthers, "Sweetness," *Speculum* 81 (2006): 1012.

5. Hugh Kenner, "Rhyme: An Unfinished Monograph," *Common Knowledge* 10 (2004): 424.

6. Ong, "Wit and Mystery," 324.

7. James Elroy Flecker, "The Old Ships," in *Collected Poems* (London: Martin Secker, 1935), 217.

8. John Masefield, "Cargoes," in *Poems* (New York: Macmillan, 1925), 117.

9. Virginia Woolf, *The Waves*, ed. James M. Haule and Philip H. Smith Jr. (Oxford: Blackwell, 1993), 20.

10. These questions are addressed in A. M. Devine and Laurence D. Stephens, *Latin Word Order: Structured Meaning and Information* (New York: Oxford University Press, 2006), 126.

11. T. S. Eliot, "Song," in *The Yale Anthology of Twentieth-Century French Poetry*, ed. Mary Ann Caws (New Haven: Yale University Press, 2004), 63.

12. George Saintsbury, *A History of English Prose Rhythm* (London: Macmillan, 1922), 472, n1.

13. All quotations from Shakespeare are from the *Complete Works*, ed. Hardin Craig and David Bevington (Glenview, Ill.: Scott Foresman, 1973).

14. Frank Kermode, *Shakespeare's Language* (New York: Farrar Straus Giroux, 2000), 227.

15. Sir Thomas Browne, *Hydriotaphia: Urn-Burial*, in *The Major Works*, ed. C. A. Patrides (London: Penguin, 1977), 269, 307–9.

16. Walter Pater, *Appreciations, with an Essay on Style* (London: Macmillan, 1889), 137.

17. Browne, *Hydriotaphia*, 310.

18. Cf. Austin Warren, *Connections* (Ann Arbor: University of Michigan Press, 1970), 11–23.

19. Sir Thomas Browne, "Of Languages," in *Works*, ed. Charles Sayle (Edinburgh: John Grant, 1927), 3: 314.

20. C. A. Patrides makes this comparison in his edition of Browne's *Major Works*, 48, n50.

21. Samuel Johnson, Prefaces, Biographical and Critical, to the Works of the English Poets, in *Works* (London: Pickering, 1825), 6: 499–500.

22. Samuel Taylor Coleridge, *Biographia Literaria*, ed. J. Shawcross (London: Oxford University Press, 1973 rpt.), 2: 10.

23. William Wordsworth, Preface to the Second Edition of *Lyrical Ballads* (1800), in *Prose Works,* ed. W. J. B. Owen and Jane Worthington Smyser (Oxford: Clarendon, 1974), 1: 148.

24. John Guillory, "It Must Be Abstract," in Frank Kermode, *Pleasure and Change: The Aesthetics of Canon,* ed. Robert Alter (New York: Oxford University Press, 2004), 65, 66.

25. Wallace Stevens, "Notes Toward a Supreme Fiction," in *Collected Poems* (New York: Vintage, 1990), 397.

26. Quoted in Bernard Weinberg, *French Realism: The Critical Reaction, 1830–1870* (New York: Oxford University Press, 1937), 165.

27. Kenneth Burke, *Counter-Statement,* 2nd ed. (Chicago: University of Chicago Press, 1957), 41.

28. Wallace Stevens, "The Comedian as the Letter C," in *Collected Poems,* 41.

29. "Le mot n'est pas la chose, mais un éclair à la lueur duquel on l'aperçoit." Quoted in Roland Barthes, *Fragments d'un discourse amoureux* (Paris: Éditions du seuil, 1977), 238.

30. Marianne Moore, *Complete Prose,* ed. Patricia C. Willis (New York: Viking, 1986), 425.

31. Marianne Moore, "Silence," in *Complete Poems* (New York: Macmillan/Viking, 1967), 91.

32. John Crowe Ransom, "The Equilibrists," in *Selected Poems* (New York: Knopf, 1963), 84.

33. Ransom, "Dead Boy," ibid., 5.

CHAPTER 3
Song Without Words

1. Maurice Blanchot, *L'Arrêt de mort* (Paris: Gallimard, 1948), 87.

2. Maurice Blanchot, *Death Sentence,* trans. Lydia Davis (Barrytown, N.Y.: Station Hill, 1978), 46 (translation slightly modified).

3. W. B. Yeats, "The Second Coming," in *The Variorum Edition of the Poems of W. B. Yeats,* ed. Peter Allt and Russell K. Alspach (New York: Macmillan, 1987), 402.

4. Alfred North Whitehead, *Adventures of Ideas* (New York: Macmillan, 1933), 173–74.

5. Friedrich Nietzsche, *On the Genealogy of Morality,* ed. Keith Ansell-Pearson, trans. Carol Diethe (Cambridge: Cambridge University Press, 1994), 57.

6. Walter Pater, *The Renaissance: Studies in Art and Poetry: The 1893 Text,* ed. Donald L. Hill (Berkeley: University of California Press, 1980), 106, 108.

7. Quoted in Geoffrey Hill, *The Lords of Limit: Essays on Literature and Ideas* (New York: Oxford University Press, 1984), 4.

8. Ibid., 9.

9. Cormac McCarthy, *Blood Meridian; or, the Evening Redness in the West* (New York: Vintage, 1992), 333, 334.

10. Herman Melville, *Moby-Dick; or, The Whale,* ed. Harrison Hayford, Hershel Parker, G. Thomas Tanselle (Evanston: Northwestern University Press, 1988), 167.

11. Samuel Taylor Coleridge, *Coleridge's Shakespearean Criticism,* ed. Thomas Middleton Raysor (Cambridge: Harvard University Press, 1930), 1: 75, 77.

12. Thomas De Quincey, *Collected Writings,* ed. David Masson (London: Black, 1897), 10: 393.

13. Gustave Flaubert, *Madame Bovary: Provincial Manners,* trans. Margaret Mauldon (Oxford: Oxford University Press, 2004), 22.

14. Gustave Flaubert, *Madame Bovary* (Paris: Flammarion, 1986 rpt.), 81.

15. Flaubert, *Madame Bovary: Provincial Manners,* 47.

16. Ibid.

17. Flaubert, *Madame Bovary,* 112.

18. Gustave Flaubert, Letter to Louise Colet, September 12, 1853, in *Correspondance* (Paris: Gallimard, 1973), 2: 429.

19. Henry James, Preface to *The American,* in *The Art of the Novel: Critical Prefaces* (New York: Scribner's, 1934), 31–32.

20. Edwin Arlington Robinson, "The Mill," in *Collected Poems* (New York: Macmillan, 1937), 460–61.

21. Emily Dickinson, Poem 591, in *The Poems of Emily Dickinson,* ed. R. W. Franklin (Cambridge: Belknap, Harvard University Press, 1999), 265–66.

22. Helen Vendler, *Poets Thinking: Pope, Whitman, Dickinson, Yeats* (Cambridge: Harvard University Press, 2004), 89.

23. Citations of the *Aeneid* in Latin are from Virgil, *Aeneid,* books IV–VI, ed. T. L. Papillon and A. E. Haigh (Oxford: Clarendon, 1890).

24. *Virgil's Aeneid,* trans. John Dryden (New York: Collier, 1909 rpt.), 227.

25. T. S. Eliot, *On Poetry and Poets* (London: Faber and Faber, 1957), 62.

CHAPTER 4
Like Something Almost Being Said

1. R. P. Blackmur, *Language as Gesture: Essays in Poetry* (New York: Harcourt, Brace, 1952), 370.

2. Martin Jacobsson, *Aurelius Augustinus, De musica liber VI* (Stockholm: Almqvist and Wiksell International, 2002).

3. W. F. Jackson Knight, *St. Augustine's De Musica: A Synopsis* (Westport, Conn.: Hyperion, 1979 rpt.), 95, 124.

4. Jacobsson, *De Musica*, 114–16.

5. Ibid., 115–17.

6. Blackmur, *Language as Gesture*, 367.

7. R. P. Blackmur, *Outsider at the Heart of Things*, ed. James T. Jones (Urbana: University of Illinois Press, 1989), 164–65.

8. Cf. Alex Ross, "American Sublime," *New Yorker*, June 19, 2006, 84–88.

9. George Eliot, *Middlemarch*, ed. Bert G. Hornback (New York: Norton, 2000), 124, 125.

10. Blackmur, *Outsider at the Heart of Things*, 170–71.

11. Quoted ibid., 170.

12. I am grateful to Peter Burian and Diskin Clay for clarifications of the issues mentioned in this paragraph.

13. Virginia Woolf, "On Not Knowing Greek," in *The Common Reader: First Series* (New York: Harcourt, Brace, 1953 rpt.), 31–32.

14. Aeschylus, *Agamemnon*, ed. Eduard Fraenkel (Oxford: Clarendon, 1950), 1: 117.

15. Aeschylus, *The Oresteia*, trans. Alan Shapiro and Peter Burian (Oxford: Oxford University Press, 2003), 58–59.

16. Henry James, "The Next Time," in *Complete Stories, 1892–1898* (New York: Library of America, 1996), 506. I have written about this story, more briefly and in another context, in *Speaking of Beauty* (New Haven: Yale University Press, 2003), 506, 510, 516, 524.

17. R. P. Blackmur, *A Primer of Ignorance*, ed. Joseph Frank (New York: Harcourt, Brace, 1967), 183, 197, 199.

18. Henry James, Preface to *The Tragic Muse*, in *The Art of the Novel: Critical Prefaces* (New York: Scribner's, 1934), 96.

19. Paul Verlaine, "Colloque sentimental," in *Selected Poems*, trans. Martin Sorrell (Oxford: Oxford University Press, 1999 rpt.), 52.

20. William Gass, *On Being Blue: A Philosophical Inquiry* (Boston: David R. Godine, 1976), 86, 89–91.

21. W. B. Yeats, "The Song of the Happy Shepherd," in *The Variorum Edition of the Poems of W. B. Yeats*, ed. Peter Allt and Russell K. Alspach (New York: Macmillan, 1987), 65.

22. Michael Fried, *Manet's Modernism; Or, the Face of Painting in the 1860s* (Chicago: University of Chicago Press, 1996), 288, 189, 196.

23. Cf. George H. W. Rylands, *Words and Poetry* (London: Hogarth, 1928), 181.

24. R. P. Blackmur, *The Lion and the Honeycomb: Essays in Solicitude and Critique* (New York: Harcourt, Brace, 1955), 292, 297.

25. Seamus Heaney, "Clearances," in *New Selected Poems, 1966–1987* (London: Faber and Faber, 1990), 232.

26. John Keats, "Ode on a Grecian Urn," in *Selected Poems and Letters*, ed. Douglas Bush (Boston: Houghton Mifflin, 1959), 207–8.

27. Kenneth Burke, *A Grammar of Motives and A Rhetoric of Motives* (Cleveland: World, 1962), 449.

28. Roland Barthes, *S/Z*, trans. Richard Miller (London: Jonathan Cape, 1975), 216–17 (translation slightly modified). Quotations in French are from Barthes, *S/Z* (Paris: Éditions du Seuil, 1970), 277.

29. Hans-Georg Gadamer, *Truth and Method*, trans. from the German; ed. Garrett Barden and John Cumming (London: Sheed and Ward, 1985 rpt.), 415–16.

30. T. S. Eliot, "Burnt Norton," in *Collected Poems, 1909–1962* (New York: Harcourt, Brace, 1963), 180.

31. Ludwig Wittgenstein, *Tractatus Logico-Philosophicus*, ed. and trans. D. F. Pears and B. F. McGuinness (London: Routledge and Kegan Paul, 1963), 151. "There are, indeed, things that cannot be put into words." I use the translation by Ken Frieden included in Jacques Derrida, "How to Avoid Speaking: Denials," *Languages of the Unsayable: The Play of Negativity in Literature and Literary Theory*, ed. Sanford Budick and Wolfgang Iser (Stanford: Stanford University Press, 1996 rpt.), 11.

32. Carol Shields, "Taking the Train," in *Collected Stories* (London: Harper Perennial, 2005), 176–77.

33. Robert Frost, "Out, Out—" in *Collected Poems, Prose, and Plays* (New York: Library of America, 1995), 131.

34. Frost, "The Unmade Word, or Fetching and Far-Fetching," ibid., 696.

1. Herman Melville, "Bartleby, the Scrivener," in *Tales, Poems, and Other Writings*, ed. John Bryant (New York: Modern Library, 2002), 95–96.

2. Ibid., 97–98.

3. Jacques Derrida, *The Gift of Death*, trans. David Wills (Chicago: University of Chicago Press, 1995), 74–75.

4. T. S. Eliot, *The Waste Land*, in *Collected Poems, 1909–1962* (New York: Harcourt Brace, 1963), 59.

5. Kenneth Burke, *Counter-Statement*, 2nd ed. (Chicago: University of Chicago Press, 1957), 31, 39.

6. Ibid., 41.

7. Kenneth Burke, *Towards a Better Life* (New York: Harcourt, Brace, 1932), xii.

8. Kenneth Burke, *Towards a Better Life*, 2nd ed. (Berkeley: University of California Press, 1966), xii–xiv.

9. Ibid., 95.

10. Kenneth Burke, *The Complete White Oxen: Collected Short Fiction* (Berkeley: University of California Press, 1968), ix.

11. Burke, *Towards a Better Life* (1966), 21–22.

12. Kenneth Burke, *Permanence and Change: An Anatomy of Purpose* (Minneapolis: Bobbs-Merrill, 1965), 50.

13. Burke, *Towards a Better Life* (1966), 211.

14. Ibid., 100–101.

15. Burke, "The Anaesthetic Revelation of Herone Liddell," in *The Complete White Oxen*, 288–89.

16. Wallace Stevens, "The Snow Man," in *The Palm at the End of the Mind*, ed. Holly Stevens (New York: Vintage, 1990), 54.

17. Stevens, "The Course of a Particular," ibid., 367.

18. Virginia Woolf, *The Waves*, ed. James M. Haule and Philip H. Smith Jr. (Oxford: Shakespeare Head by Blackwell, 1993), 190.

19. James Wood, *The Broken Estate: Essays on Literature and Belief* (London: Jonathan Cape, 1999), 103: "Bernard, at the end of *The Waves*, does not give a Paterian account of the primacy of art, or the ultimate aesthetic pattern of all things (the usual reading), but rather, he undergoes a breakdown which is described in spiritual terms."

20. Woolf, *The Waves*, 190.

CHAPTER 6

Blind Mouths

1. Charles Rosen, "From the Troubadours to Frank Sinatra," *New York Review of Books*, February 23, 2006, 43.

2. T. W. Adorno, "The Handle, the Pot, and Early Experience," in *Notes to Literature: Volume Two*, trans. Shierry Weber Nicholsen (New York: Columbia University Press, 1992), 218.

3. Dante Alighieri, *La Divina Commedia*, ed. C. H. Grandgent, rev. Charles S. Singleton (Cambridge: Harvard University Press, 1972), 635.

4. Ovid, *Metamorphoses*, trans. F. J. Miller (Cambridge: Harvard University Press, 1968), 2: 292–94.

5. Hugh Kenner, "Rhyme: An Unfinished Monograph," *Common Knowledge* 10 (2004): 414.

6. Dante, "Letter X to Can Grande de la Scala," trans. Robert S. Haller in *Literary Criticism of Dante Alighieri* (Lincoln: University of Nebraska Press, 1973), 110. (The authenticity of this letter is still in dispute.)

7. Hilary of Poitiers, *De Trinitate*, lib. 2, n5, quoted in Walter J. Ong, "Wit and Mystery: A Revaluation in Medieval Latin Hymnody," *Speculum* 22 (1947): 337, n68.

8. Cf. Kenner, "Rhyme," 549–50.

9. T. S. Eliot, "'Rhetoric' and Poetic Drama," in *Selected Essays* (New York: Harcourt, Brace, 1950), 27.

10. Cf. Kenner, "Rhyme," 420.

11. Ezra Pound, *The Cantos of Ezra Pound* (New York: New Directions, 1993), 549.

12. Walter Benjamin, *One-Way Street and Other Writings*, trans. Edmund Jephcott and Kingsley Shorter (London: Verso, 1979), 95.

13. Geoffrey Hill, "Style and Faith," *Times Literary Supplement*, December 27, 1991, 3–4.

14. Adorno, *Notes to Literature: Volume Two*, 287, 289.

15. Walter Benjamin, *The Origin of German Tragic Drama*, trans. John Osborne (London: Verso, 1998 rpt.), 166.

16. Benjamin, *One-Way Street*, 70–71.

17. Paul de Man, *Blindness and Insight: Essays in the Rhetoric of Contemporary Criticism*, 2nd ed., rev. (Minneapolis: University of Minnesota Press, 1983), 191. For a critique of de Man on the symbol, see David Lloyd, "Kant's Examples," *Representations*, no. 28 (1989): 34–54.

18. John Locke, *An Essay Concerning Human Understanding*, ed. John W. Yolton (London: Dent, 1968 rpt.), 2: book 3, chapter 10, 104.

19. Ibid., 97.

20. E. M. Cioran, *The Temptation to Exist,* trans. Richard Howard (Chicago: Quadrangle, 1968), 126–27.

21. John Milton, "Lycidas," in *Works,* ed. Frank Allen Patterson et al. (New York: Columbia University Press, 1931), 1: part 1, 80–81.

22. John Ruskin, *Sesame and Lilies . . . Unto This Last . . . The Queen of the Air . . . The Storm Cloud of the Nineteenth Century* (Boston: Dana Estes, n.d.), 47.

23. William Empson, "This Last Pain," in *Collected Poems* (New York: Harcourt, Brace, 1949), 34.

24. Ludwig Wittgenstein, *Tractatus Logico-Philosophicus,* quoted in Philip Gardner and Averil Gardner, *The God Approached: A Commentary on the Poems of William Empson* (London: Chatto and Windus, 1978), 123.

25. Søren Kierkegaard, *Either/Or,* trans. D. F. Swenson and L. M. Swenson (New York: Anchor, 1959), 1: 143.

CHAPTER 7

For and Against

Epigraph. Augustine's Latin reads: "Sunt etiam quaedam praecepta uberioris disputationis quae iam eloquentia nominator, quae nihilominus vera sunt, quamvis eis possint etiam falsa persuaderi." The translation is from *De Doctrina Christiana,* ed. and trans. R. P. H. Green (Oxford: Clarendon, 1995), 118.

1. John Milton, *Paradise Regained,* in *Complete Poems and Major Prose,* ed. Merritt Y. Hughes (New York: Odyssey, 1957), 487.

2. John Donne, *The Sermons of John Donne,* ed. George R. Potter and Evelyn M. Simpson (Berkeley: University of California Press, 1953–1962), 6: 55. Quoted in part in Geoffrey Hill, *Style and Faith* (New York: Counterpoint,2003), 100.

3. Hill, *Style and Faith,* 54–55.

4. David Bromwich, *Skeptical Music: Essays on Modern Poetry* (Chicago: University of Chicago Press, 2001), 152.

5. Tzvetan Todorov, *Mikhail Bakhtin: The Dialogical Principle,* trans. Wlad Godzich (Minneapolis: University of Minnesota Press, 1984), x.

6. Ezra Pound, *The Cantos of Ezra Pound* (New York: New Directions, 1996), 135.

7. Virginia Woolf, *To the Lighthouse,* ed. Mark Hussey (Orlando: Harcourt, 2005 rpt.), 112–13.

8. Michel de Montaigne, *Les Essais*, ed. Claude Pinganaud (Paris: Arléa, 1992), 194.

9. Samuel Johnson, Preface to *A Dictionary of the English Language* (1755), in *Johnson on the English Language*, ed. Gwin J. Kolb and Robert Demaria Jr. (New Haven: Yale University Press, 2005), 79.

10. Cf. Leo Bersani, "Against *Ulysses*," *Raritan* 8, no. 2 (1988): 15: "In *Bouvard et Pécuchet*, style caresses an encyclopedic culture out of its projects of mastery, into a liberalizing impotence."

11. Edmund Burke, *Reflections on the Revolution in France*, ed. Frank Turner (New Haven: Yale University Press, 2003 rpt.), 65. Philip Francis to Edmund Burke, February 19, 1790, in Edmund Burke, *Correspondence*, ed. Thomas W. Copeland et al. (Cambridge: Cambridge University Press, 1958–78), 6: 86.

12. Kenneth Burke, *Permanence and Change: An Anatomy of Purpose*, 2nd rev. ed. (Indianapolis: Bobbs-Merrill, 1965 rpt.), 50.

13. Cf. Mario Untersteiner, *The Sophists*, trans. Kathleen Freeman (Oxford: Blackwell, 1954), 107.

14. Cf. Bruce W. Winter, *Philo and Paul Among the Sophists: Alexandrian and Corinthian Responses to a Julio-Claudian Movement*, 2nd ed. (Grand Rapids, Mich.: Eerdmans, 2002), 180–93.

15. Robert Graves, "The Cool Web," in *New Collected Poems* (Garden City, N.Y.: Doubleday, 1977), 27.

16. Ibid.

17. Theodore Roethke, "Open House," in *Collected Poems* (Garden City, New York: Doubleday, 1966), 3.

18. T. S. Eliot, in *The Athenaeum*, April 11, 1919, quoted in Christopher Ricks, Introduction to Samuel Menashe, *New and Selected Poems* (New York: Library of America, 2005), xxxvi.

19. Ibid.

20. John Donne, "Litanie," in *The Complete English Poems*, ed. A. J. Smith (New York: St. Martin's, 1971), 323.

21. Cf. Helen Peters, Introduction to her edition of John Donne, *Paradoxes and Problems* (Oxford: Clarendon, 1980), xxvii–xxviii.

22. Donne, *Paradoxes and Problems*, 33–35.

23. James Joyce, *Finnegans Wake* (New York: Penguin, 1999 rpt.), 14.

24. John Locke, *An Essay Concerning Human Understanding*, ed. John W. Yolton (London: Dent; New York: Dutton, 1968 rpt.), 2: 104–5.

25. Cf. Jeremy Waldron, *God, Locke, and Equality: Christian Foundations of John Locke's Political Thought* (Cambridge: Cambridge University Press, 2002), 23–25.

26. Philip Sidney, *Defence of Poesie,* in *Defence of Poesie, Astrophil and Stella, and Other Writings,* ed. Elizabeth Porges Watson (London: Everyman, 1997), 125. "Coursing of a letter" refers to excessive, pedantic alliteration. "Method of a Dictionary" is to choose words merely as they appear under any one letter of the alphabet. Sidney parodies these habits of style in *Astrophil and Stella,* 15.

27. Samuel Beckett, *Malone Dies,* trans. by the author (New York: Grove, 1970 rpt.), 19.

28. Samuel Beckett, "The End," in *First Love and Other Novellas,* ed. Gerry Dukes (London: Penguin, 2000 rpt.), 29.

29. Edmund Husserl, "The Origin of Geometry," appendix 6 in *The Crisis of European Sciences and Transcendental Phenomenology: An Introduction to Phenomenological Philosophy,* trans. David Carr (Evanston: Northwestern University Press, 1970), 362, 367.

30. Jacques Derrida, *Edmund Husserl's Origin of Geometry: An Introduction,* trans. John P. Leavey Jr. (Lincoln: University of Nebraska Press, 1978), 82, 104. Derrida's further commentary on "The Origin of Geometry" is in *The Problem of Genesis in Husserl's Philosophy,* trans. Marian Hobson (Chicago: University of Chicago Press, 2003), 161–69.

31. Edmund Husserl, "Philosophy as Rigorous Science," 144, quoted in Derrida, *Edmund Husserl's Origin of Geometry,* 101, n109.

32. Ibid., 101, 102.

33. John Donne, "Epithalamion at the Marriage of the Earl of Somerset," in *The Epithalamions, Anniversaries, and Epicedes,* ed. W. Milgate (Oxford: Clarendon, 1978), 13.

34. Kenneth Burke, *Counter-Statement,* 2nd ed. (Chicago: University of Chicago Press, 1957), 166–68.

35. John Donne, "The Exstasie," in *The Elegies and the Songs and Sonnets,* ed. Helen Gardner (Oxford: Clarendon, 2000 rpt.), 65. Gardner's emendation of *Which* to *That* has not generally (or here) been accepted.

36. Paul Muldoon, "Sillyhow Stride," *Times Literary Supplement,* June 2, 2006, 7.

37. Donne, *Elegies and the Songs and Sonnets,* 265.

38. John Donne, *Letters to Severall Persons of Honour,* 46. Quoted in Milgate, *Epithalamions, Anniversaries, and Epicedes,* xvi.

39. Donne, *Elegies and the Songs and Sonnets,* 260.

40. William Empson, *Essays on Renaissance Literature,* ed. John Haffenden (Cambridge: Cambridge University Press, 1993), 1: 158.

41. Wallace Stevens, "The Motive for Metaphor," in *Collected Poems* (New York: Vintage, 1990), 288.

42. Theodor W. Adorno, *Aesthetic Theory*, trans. Robert Hullot-Kentor (Minneapolis: University of Minnesota Press, 1997), 237.

43. Hullot-Kentor, translator's note, ibid., 371.

44. T. S. Eliot, "Andrew Marvell," in *Selected Essays* (New York: Harcourt, Brace, and World, 1964), 252.

45. Woolf, *To the Lighthouse*, 121. The line of verse is from William Browne's "The Inner Temple Masque."

46. William Shakespeare, Sonnet 98, in *Complete Works*, ed. Hardin Craig and David Bevington (Glenview, Ill.: Scott, Foresman, 1973), 487.

47. Woolf, *To the Lighthouse*, 123.

48. Ibid., 124.

INDEX

lamion at the Marriage of the Earl of Somerset," 168–69; "The Exstasie," 170–71; letter to Sir Henry Goodyer, 171–72; "Litanie," 159; *Paradoxes and Problems,* 159–61, 164

Dostoevsky, Fyodor, 81

Douay Old Testament, 5

Dryden, John, 67–68

Dunning, T. P., 29

Egotism, 169

Eliot, George, *Middlemarch,* 76–79, 81, 85

Eliot, T. S., 13, 28, 74, 86, 156; *Ara Vos Prec,* 128; "Ash Wednesday," 49, 128, 131–32; "Burnt Norton," 95; "Chanson" translated by, 27; *Four Quartets,* 49; "Gerontion," 149; on "incantation," 64; "Marina," 3–4; on Marvell's poetry, 174; "Poetry and Drama," 48–49; on Shakespeare, 128; on simplicity, 157–58; and Symbolism, 168; *The Use of Poetry and the Use of Criticism,* 47; *The Waste Land,* 106–8, 132; "What Is a Classic?," 68, 69

Elizabethan song, 167

Ellis, Havelock, 20

Eloquence: of ambience, 158–59; arguments for and against, 145–49, 152, 158–72; in endings, 115–21, 122, 123, 129–31; excess of saying as, 140, 142, 154, 158; as a factor added to life, 41, 148; grandiloquence vs., 41–42; indifference to, 19; in language, *see* Language; larger perspective in, 103; meanings of the

term, 112, 148; in the mind's outer limits, 122, 125, 132; moral indifference of, 158–59, 161, 164; personification of, 163–64; rejection of, 143–45; rhetoric vs., 3–4, 112, 148; social and cultural, 59; in transitions, 108–15; as a value, 152; won from language, 133

Elton, Charles, "Luriana, Lurilee," 151

Emerson, Ralph Waldo, 28; Divinity School Address, 99

Empson, William, 103, 172; *Seven Types of Ambiguity,* 82–83; "This Last Pain," 140–41

Emptiness, 90–91

Endings, 115–21, 122, 123, 129–31

English language: civic (middle) style, 156; corruption of, 6, 10–11, 12; decline of, 8–12; formal, 114; held in low esteem, 4–5; Johnson's dictionary of, 9–11, 151; Latin influence on, 27, 29–32; in political speeches, 7–8; refinement of, 5–6; social class reflected in, 7, 8–9; in translations, 5, 11; vernacular, 4, 12; written, 13

Enlightenment, 12

Equivocation, 166–67

Erasmus, 5

Etymology, 30, 132

Euripides, 80

Fallacy, 163

Fantin-Latour, Henri, *Woman Reading,* 88

Feldman, Morton, 76

Figures of speech, 127, 161–63

the blue," 83–86; "The Death of the Lion," 85; "The Figure in the Carpet," 85; "The Great Good Place," 85; "The Lesson of the Master," 85; "The Next Time," 83–85; *The Portrait of a Lady*, 76; "The Private Life," 85; on pulp fiction, 12; on real vs. romantic, 60–61; *The Tragic Muse*, 86

James, Saint, 42

Jesus Christ, 143–45

Johnson, Samuel: *A Dictionary of the English Language*, 9–11, 151; *The Lives of the English Poets*, 36–38

Jonson, Ben, 29; *Sejanus*, 32–33

Joyce, James: *Dubliners*, 47; equivocation in works of, 166–67; *Finnegans Wake*, 2, 47, 137, 147, 161, 166; *A Portrait of the Artist as a Young Man*, 21, 47; *Ulysses*, 22, 47, 147, 166

Kafka, Franz: *Metamorphosis*, 137; *The Castle*, 62–64

Keats, John, 12, 115; "Ode on a Grecian Urn," 91, 92

Kennedy, John F., 7

Kenner, Hugh, 23–24, 124, 132, 167–68

Kermode, Frank, 30

Kierkegaard, Søren, *Either/Or*, 141

King, Martin Luther, Jr., 7; "Letter from a Birmingham Jail," 147–48

King James Bible, 5

Knight, W. F. Jackson, *St. Augustine's De Musica: A Synopsis*, 71

Kyd, Thomas, *The Spanish Tragedy*, 132

Landor, Walter Savage, 28

Langer, Susanne, 41

Language: ambiguity of, 80–81, 82–83; Anglo-Saxon, 31; autonomy of, 2; being alive in, 40; of Bibles, 5–6; in Book of Genesis, 129–30; catachresis of, 135–40; commercial, 18–19; corruption of, 6–7, 10–11, 12; creative power of, 49, 136; declining quality of, 8–12; English, *see* English language; estranging disposition of, 133; etymology, 30, 132; expectations in, 132; expressive, 94; figurative, 111; foreign phrases inserted into, 131–34; Greek, 42, 80–83; Hebrew, 80, 126; high style of, 7; impartial, 57–62; Latin, *see* Latin language; limitations of, 81, 123–29, 136, 157, 169; "little," 121; mastery of, 134–35, 137; meaning on far side of, 81, 82–83; of music, 123; nonverbal, 49–51, 57, 64, 75–76, 93–96; outer limits of, 140–41; proper vs. improper, 164–65; referential act of, 1–2; representational, 136; salvation in, 123; seduction of, 165, 167; sin of, 157–58; standards of, 12; tower of Babel, 75, 126, 130; transcending, 155, 165–66; translations of, 5, 11, 72–74, 81, 83, 166; univocity of, 165–68; Ur-language, 80; of wartime speeches, 7; words in, *see* Words

Picasso, Pablo, 135
Pius VII, Pope, 21
Plato, 125
Player, The (film), 170
Poe, Edgar Allan, 28, 48, 49
Poetry, language of, 49
Positivism, 41
Possibility, 141
Pound, Ezra, 148, 156, 168; *Cantos,* 128–29, 149
Prudence, 157

Quintilian, 5
Quotations, 132–33

Ransom, John Crowe, 93; "Dead Boy," 42; "The Equilibrists," 42
Realism, 60–61, 136
Renaissance, 5
Rhetoric: eloquence as different from, 3–4, 148; meaning of the term, 112, 148; of public speaking, 7–8, 159
Rhythm, 71–76
Rice, Edmund Ignatius, 21
Ricks, Christopher, 158
Rilke, Rainer Maria, 31; *Neue Gedichte,* 133
Robinson, Edwin Arlington, "The Mill," 62–64
Roethke, Theodore, "Open House," 157
Roman Catholic Church, Latin ritual of, 22, 23–24, 42
Romanticism, 61
Rome, classics of, 5, 7
Rosen, Charles, 123
Rote learning, 157
Ruskin, John, 139–40
Russell, Bertrand, 158

Sainte-Beuve, Charles-Augustin, 41
Saintsbury, George, *History of English Prose Rhythm,* 27–28
Sands, Bobby, 105
Schoenberg, Arnold, 134
Scott, Sir Walter, *The Antiquary,* 174
Semple, Patrick, 26, 27
Sequence, eloquence of, 55–56
Shakespeare, William, 3, 34, 80, 81; *Antony and Cleopatra,* 29–30, 31; *Coriolanus,* 128, 148; *Hamlet,* 87–90, 107, 135, 155; *Henry VIII,* 30; *King Lear,* 13–14, 32, 43, 121, 130; *Macbeth,* 30, 51–56, 137–38; *Measure for Measure,* 149; *Othello,* 128, 131; "sonnet 98," 175–76; *The Tempest,* 30; *Timon of Athens,* 128
Shapiro, Alan, 82
Shelley, Percy Bysshe, "Ode to the West Wind," 117
Shields, Carol, "Taking the Train," 96–98
Sidney, Philip, *Defence of Poesie,* 164
Silence, 48, 50–51; above silence, 92; after the words have stopped, 74–75; forever, 92; of gesture, 75–76, 93; interpretation of, 76–79, 82–83; rhythm of, 75–76; of something almost being said, 79, 91–93, 94–95, 98
Sonority, 167
Sophocles, 80
Southwell, Robert, "Marie Magdalens Funeral Teares," 149
Speech: against the grain, 133; charisma of, 146; elegance of,

imagination and, 71; inner dimension of, 94–95; lack of, 127; as mantra, 74; and music, 5–6, 167; necessity of, 123; out of context, 44–47, 69, 148–49, 171, 172; perception of, 41, 78; in phrases, 120–21, 131–34; responsiveness to, 19–20; silence after, 74–75; songs without, 48, 49–51, 56–58, 61–64, 66–69, 76; as words, 115, 117, 166

Wordsworth, William: *Lyrical Ballads,* 11–12, 38, 39; "Michael," 4

Wright, James, "Lying in a Ham-

mock at William Duffy's Farm in Pine Island, Minnesota," 31

Writing: aims of, 170; qualities of, 13

Yeats, William Butler, 13, 48, 120; "Down by the Salley Gardens," 129; "Long-Legged Fly," 95; "No Second Troy," 14; "The Second Coming," 45–46, 135; "The Song of the Happy Shepherd," 87; and Symbolism, 168; writing method of, 108